BernNadette Stanis
with Brittany Rose

Copyright © 2024 by BernNadette Stanis
All rights reserved. Printed in the United States of America

Published by:
The Worthingham Group, LLC
8306 Wilshire Boulevard
Beverly Hills, California 90211

This is a work of creative non-fiction. All of the events in this memoir are true to the best of the author's memory. Some names and identifying features have been changed to protect the identity of certain parties. The author in no way represents any company, corporation, or brand mentioned herein. The views expressed in this memoir are solely those of the author.

For privacy reasons, some names, locations, and dates may have been changed.

No part of this publication may be reproduced, distributed, or transmitted in any form or by any means, including photocopying, recording, or other electronic or mechanical methods, without the prior written permission of the publisher, except as permitted by U.S. copyright law. For permission requests, contact The Worthingham Group at Classicartists1@gmail.com.

ISBN: 978-0-9770361-7-2 (paperback)
ISBN: 978-0-9770361-8-9 (hardcover)

Book Cover and Interior Design by
Jessica Tilles/TWA Solutions & Services

Worldwide Distribution by
Ingram Content Group
www.ingramcontent.com

For more information on BernNadette Stanis, visit her online:
https://www.thelmaofgoodtimes.com/
Follow her on social media:
Facebook: @Bern Nadette Stanis
Instagram: @thelmaofgoodtimes
Twitter: @thelmagoodtimes

TO ALL OF MY...

Incredible fans who have stood by me through every chapter of my life and career, this book is for you. Your unwavering support, kind words, and heartfelt messages—whether in person or on social media—mean the world to me. I read every comment and letter, and each one fills my heart with joy and inspiration. As we celebrate fifty years of *Good Times* (1974–2024), I can't think of a better way to honor this golden anniversary than by sharing my journey with you. I hope you enjoy reading it as much as I have cherished writing it for you. Thank you for being part of this beautiful ride and holding me close to your heart.

Other Titles by BernNadette Stanis

The Last Night: A Caregivers Journey Through Transition and Beyond

Situations 101 Relationships: The Good, The Bad & The Ugly

Situations 101 Finances: The Good, The Bad & The Ugly

For Men Only

Acknowledgments

Mayor Van Johnson

Kevin Fontana

Frederick Williams

Patricia Edwards

Rebecca Whildin

Trent T. Daniel

My daughters: Dior Ravel and Brittany Rose

My granddaughters: Leto MaNon and Eulilia Mae

My siblings: Pastor Gregory Kyle, Talbert Kethrell, Deborah Louise, and Yolanda Stanislaus

My parents: Gregory Talbert and Eula Stanislaus

Table of Contents

Preface: A Symphony of Golden Moments xiii
Introduction: Good Times—Historical Context......... 1
   A Movement in Prime Time: Civil Rights
     Reflected in *Good Times* 3
Chapter 1 - From Brooklyn to Hollywood Early Life:
   Family and Community..11
     Cinderella in the Ghetto: The Road to Thelma......... 16
Chapter 2 - Let the Good Times Roll 24
     First Impressions 24
     Developing Thelma..27
     Esther Rolle: A Motherly Force On and Off the
       Good Times Set..31
     Lifelong Friends 37
     Damn, Damn, Damn!..40
Chapter 3 - Kings of the Set: My *Good Times*
   Costars..42
     John Amos..42
     Jimmie Walker...50
     Dyn-O-Mite! 54
     Big Brother..56
     Ralph Carter..59
Chapter 4 – Familiar Faces..65
     Ja'Net DuBois: Everyone's Favorite Neighbor..........65

Ben Powers: Selecting My Husband 70
The Wedding 70
The Vows 72
Janet Jackson: A Legend in the Making 74
Johnny Brown (Buffalo Butt) 78
Sweet Daddy Williams: The Menacing
    Numbers Runner 80
Looting Lenny: The Character Within a
    Character 83
Moses Gunn as Carl Dixon 84
Chip Fields: From Auditioning for Thelma to
    Portraying an Iconic Character 85

**Chapter 5 – The Minds Behind the Magic: The
Creative Team 87**
The Creators: Eric Monte and Michael Evans 87
Norman Lear: The Visionary Producer 90
A Consummate Professional 92
Guiding the Moments: The Directors Who Shaped
    Good Times.. 96
Herbert Kenwith 96
Gerren Keith 100
Allan Manings: A Legacy in Television
    Comedy 102
Writers 104

Chapter 6 - Cameos and Connections: The Stars Who Graced Our Stage 105
   Comedy Behind the Scenes: Jay Leno's Stand-Up Visit 105
   Comedy Quartet 107
   A Childhood Star All Grown Up Stymie Beard's Return to the Screen 109
   Roscoe Lee Browne: A Poignant Presence as Reverend Sam 110
   A Memorable Collaboration with Philip Michael Thomas 112
   Johnny Sekka's Royal Presence 115
   Challenging Stereotypes and Celebrating Africa 116
   African Culture Brought to Life 117
   Sassy and Sharp: Helen Martin 118
   Raymond Allen as Ned the Wino 120

Chapter 7 - The Brush, Rhythm, and Wardrobe: Coloring the Soul of *Good Times* 123
   Ernie Barnes: The Artist Who Painted Our World 123
   Adella Farmar: Fashionista 127
   Jim Gilstrap: Singer 130
   Sondra "Blinky" Williams: Singer 133
   Dave Grusin: Composer 134

Alan and Marilyn Bergman: Lyricists 135
Good Times Theme Song Lyrics............................... 137
Chapter 8 – Behind the Scenes with Thelma: Your Questions Answered 138
Character Insights and Personal Experiences 138
Fan Encounters and Reactions 145
Set and Cast Dynamics 150
Hollywood Realities and Opportunities 153
Chapter 9 - Personal Reflections 158
Beauty – An original poem by BernNadette........... 161
Chapter 10 - A Cultural Impact Beyond the Screen 164
That's A Wrap! - Words of Wisdom for Future Generations 167
What Would I Tell the Younger Me? 168
Captured Moments: My Life in Pictures 171
Script: BernNadette's Original Script 247

About BernNadette Stanis 297
About Brittany Rose... 298

PREFACE

A Symphony of Golden Moments

The very first time our television family—Esther Rolle, John Amos, Jimmie Walker, Ralph Carter, Ja'Net DuBois, and I—walked onto the set and recorded the pilot episode of *Good Times*, we did not know it would become a cultural phenomenon. From 1974 to 1979, for five years of Thursday nights, we offered the country a different portrayal of the Black family, one that challenged the narrative society had long perpetuated. We presented a traditional family with two parents in the household: a father who did his best to provide for his wife and children, and a mother whose maternal instincts guided her in protecting them as best she could.

Being cast as Thelma Ann Evans, the teenage daughter, was one of the greatest honors of my life. It was the first time a television series featured a young Black girl. *Good Times* represented several groundbreaking firsts for Black people in the media, all of which played an integral role in this story.

One of our greatest achievements was the positive impact we had on the Black community. We had just emerged from the turbulent 1960s, a period marked by the assassinations of two of our heroes, Dr. Martin Luther King Jr. and Malcolm X, along with the brutal murder of four little girls at the Sixteenth Baptist Church in Birmingham, Alabama. Our community needed something to elevate our collective spirit and foster a more positive consciousness—and we served that purpose.

In this book, I have attempted to capture the history of those five years. I write about my experiences as a young Black girl from the Van Dyke Projects in the Brownsville community of Brooklyn, New York, to the bright lights of Hollywood. Over the past year, I have spent time researching, reminiscing, and ultimately writing about my journey on the set of *Good Times*, while also offering a closer look at the other important people involved in the show. Most importantly, I have documented our legacy for the history books, ensuring that future generations will know and appreciate what we achieved.

As a young teenager during this time, I was transitioning into adulthood. Reflecting on my early 1970s experiences, I liken it to a modern-day Cinderella tale set against the backdrop of the urban ghetto. It was a narrative accompanied by a melodic symphony of soundtracks, with each song representing a poignant chapter in the story of a "ghetto

Cinderella." Of all the melodies that colored those formative years, Donnie Hathaway's "The Ghetto" remains a timeless anthem, transporting me back to moments of pure joy, where my mother's living room became a stage for uninhibited expression. Songs like Stevie Wonder's "You Are the Sunshine of My Life" evoke the nostalgia and warmth that defined those golden days.

INTRODUCTION

Good Times—Historical Context

Let me take you back to the good ol' days of *Good Times* when I had the chance to be part of something extraordinary. You know, it's incredible to think that we were the first show on television to feature a fully Black family with a mom and a dad. That was a big deal, and we have Esther Rolle to thank for bringing such dignity and reality to our screens. When the producers wanted to make her character a single mom on her own show, she put her foot down. She insisted that Florida have a husband and a father for her three kids. Esther wanted to show the world that Black men stood by their families, just like in any other culture. You know what? I couldn't agree more. I grew up with my mom and dad, so I'm glad Esther stuck to her principles.

Esther Rolle was a force to be reckoned with. She had strong morals and made sure they came through in every episode. When John Amos learned about Esther's concerns regarding the show, he didn't hesitate to support her. He even jokingly hinted, "Let me be your husband," and she said, "Okay."

When Esther was asked who she wanted as her husband on the show, she didn't hesitate. "I want John Amos."

Before *Good Times*, there was nothing quite like it on television. Esther and John watched over the show with great care, understanding how important it was to get things right—even if it meant having tough conversations. And let me tell you, navigating those waters wasn't easy, especially in the 1970s. That was a time of change, coming out of the 1960s, when Black people were starting to make their mark on the world.

Our leading lady, Esther, embodied the role of Florida Evans with a deep understanding of the state of African Americans in America during that era. The show's debut on February 8, 1974, amid the aftershocks of the Civil Rights

Movement and the assassination of Dr. Martin Luther King Jr., held particular significance. America was grappling with its identity, and *Good Times* emerged as a mirror reflecting the lives of African American families, especially those living in the Cabrini-Green projects of Chicago, Illinois.

A Movement in Prime Time: Civil Rights Reflected in Good Times

Good Times was born from the struggles and triumphs of the Civil Rights Movement. Black Americans were fighting for their lives, their voices, and their right to be seen and valued. The show, alongside *Sanford and Son* and *The Jeffersons*, elevated Black experiences to mainstream media. The senseless deaths of activists who carried on Dr. King's message paved the way for unprecedented levels of Black representation we saw at that time. In a television landscape dominated by all-white casts, often featuring Black actors only in minor roles, *Good Times* became a groundbreaking cultural moment. Our cast took this responsibility seriously, bringing authenticity to our characters and portraying what it meant to be Black in 1970s America.

The show was the product of the hard-won victories of civil rights activists. Without the Civil Rights Act of 1964 and the tireless efforts of those who fought for its enforcement, *Good Times* would never have reached its groundbreaking status. Reflecting on my experiences, I cannot separate the success of the show from the struggles and sacrifices that made it possible.

The 1960s were a turbulent decade, marked by violence and loss. We witnessed the assassinations of President John F. Kennedy in 1963, Dr. Martin Luther King Jr. in 1968, and Robert F. Kennedy that same year. I remember vividly sitting in Catholic Mass when I learned the news of President Kennedy having received a fatal gunshot wound to the head. Black America mourned deeply, as many of us saw him as an ally who understood our struggles. Even as a child, I sensed the uncertainty and unrest that followed.

On July 2, 1964, Dr. King stood with President Lyndon B. Johnson as he signed the Civil Rights Act. This landmark legislation made segregation in public spaces and hiring discrimination illegal, paving the way for the Voting Rights Act of 1965. The Voting Rights Act ensured Black Americans could exercise their right to vote, banning literacy tests and other discriminatory practices designed to suppress Black voters.

However, these rights came at great cost. The pushback was immense, and passing laws didn't guarantee their enforcement. Many refused to comply, leading to protests and activism throughout the decade. In the spring of 1968, Dr. King's assassination triggered riots across the country. That summer, Robert F. Kennedy, a friend of Dr. King and a supporter of civil rights, was assassinated while campaigning for president in Los Angeles. The nation fought against an ideology that denied freedom and equality for all, and at times, it felt like that ideology might prevail.

Yet, this tumultuous period laid the groundwork for shows like *Good Times*, *The Jeffersons*, *All in the Family*, and *The Cosby Show*. The Civil Rights Movement gave Black America a voice, and we used it! As an ally, producer Norman Lear saw an opportunity to amplify those voices and introduce Black families to mainstream audiences. Norman didn't shy away from hiring strong, outspoken Black actors like Esther Rolle and John Amos, who fought against stereotypes and championed authentic portrayals.

As the first African American sitcom centered on a two-parent household, *Good Times* carried both the weight and privilege of representation. Our episodes tackled many issues addressed in the Civil Rights Movement, including systemic racism, economic inequality, gang violence, prison reform, drug addiction, and more. Norman Lear constantly battled network censors who wanted to silence us, but we got our message out.

That is why *Good Times* meant so much to us and Black audiences everywhere. It wasn't just a TV show—it was a reflection of our lives, struggles, and victories. People connected to the stories, which is why the show remained relevant for generations. It wasn't just about entertainment; it was about telling our truth and showing the world who we were.

Decades later, the impact of the Civil Rights Movement and shows like *Good Times* can still be felt. Thirty-four years after our show first aired, Barack Hussein Obama became the first African American President of the United States. As of this writing, the first African American woman and the current Vice President of the United States, Kamala Devi Harris, is running for president. These are the victories and representation we fought for.

Looking ahead, I want younger generations to understand the history of the Civil Rights Movement—its triumphs and the work that remains. I had the honor of walking the historical Edmund Pettus Bridge in Selma, Alabama, on the fiftieth anniversary of the Selma to Montgomery march. It filled me with pride to see so many young people there. Educate yourselves on the movement and why it still matters. Speak with your family and community members who lived through that time. Many of the freedoms and opportunities you have today were won during the 1960s and 1970s, but the fight didn't end there. We pass the torch to future generations to uphold and expand civil rights. Every generation brings its unique skills to the cause. Make sure that good times are here to stay.

Good Times, Ain't We Lucky We Got 'Em:
Memoir of an American Sweetheart

Good Times, Ain't We Lucky We Got 'Em:
Memoir of an American Sweetheart

BernNadette Stanis with Brittany Rose

genius who ended
blackout on blacks

...ing 3rd from left) joins cast of "Good Times" in a break between shooting in studio as BerNadette Stanis gives Jimmie Walker an ...races. In group are (l to r) Ralph Carter, Director Herbert Kenwick, Lear, Esther Rolle, John Amos and Producer Allan Mannings.

TRUBO

many years since   years since television began. He launched a   "Good Times," "The Jeffersons," and

CHAPTER 1

From Brooklyn to Hollywood
Early Life: Family and Community

There are many similarities between *Good Times* and my upbringing. Growing up in Brooklyn, New York, in the Van Dyke projects in Brownsville, alongside my siblings—Gregory, Talbert, Deborah, and Yolanda—life in Brownsville was something special. While some might think living in a neighborhood like that was tough, it was where we thrived. Brownsville wasn't just where we lived; it was where our whole crew hung out, surrounded by love. Outsiders might not understand our attachment to such a rough neighborhood, but it gave us a deep sense of community, love, and tight-knit friendships.

My parents, Gregory and Eula Stanislaus, played a significant role in creating an upbringing that felt safe and full of possibilities. Blessed with the guidance of their love, I moved through my adolescence with strength and a sense

My parents, Gregory and Eula Stanislaus

My siblings (L to R) Kethrell, Yolanda, Gregory, BernNadette, Debbie

of freedom—a testament to their unchanging support. Though my mother's rules were firm, they were tempered with compassion and understanding, creating a nurturing environment that encouraged individual expression and talent. My father, with his steady presence and paternal wisdom, shaped our family dynamic. Together, they provided the foundation we needed to traverse the challenges of our surroundings, instilling in us a sense of purpose and discipline that extended to both academic and extracurricular pursuits.

Education emerged as our sanctuary, guided by my father's mantra: "What's around you does not have to be in you." With determination and resolve, we pressed forward, armed with the belief that success was not merely a distant dream but an achievable reality.

The symphony of golden moments that filled our upbringing is a testament to my parents' devotion, love, and sacrifice. In the crucible of the 1970s, amid societal upheaval and urban challenges, my parents emerged as beacons of strength, guiding us through. They instilled in us the belief that we could accomplish anything we set our minds to, and this mindset stayed with us well into adulthood. It gave us the courage to dream big and confront life's challenges head-on. Our dreams were more than just idle wishes; we fueled them with hard work, discipline, and a strong sense of self-worth.

Mom was our rock, always finding the silver lining in every situation. She also had a knack for sniffing out trouble from a mile away and steering us clear without missing a beat. Through thick and thin, she held our family together, never complaining and consistently guiding us with grace.

A true crusader for justice, Dad couldn't stand to see anyone mistreated. Our community admired him as a dedicated activist of his time. His motto was "Help somebody," and he truly lived by it.

He worked alongside leaders such as Shirley Chisholm and other community figures to improve our neighborhood. Dad taught young men to communicate their needs effectively and achieve their goals, and mentored individuals like Reverend Al Sharpton.

Dad was also a musician and belonged to a band, and I remember tagging along with him to band rehearsal when I was about three years old. I'd watch him play the saxophone with such passion that it was contagious. That's probably where I got my love for dancing, too. Dancing always felt like freedom, which is likely why I love listening to the saxophone today. Whenever I hear its sound, I want to dance, and it brings back cherished memories of those early days with Dad.

Mom's and Dad's wisdom, along with the love and honesty they showed us, shaped who we became. Despite the surrounding challenges, such as drugs and gangs, we remained true to ourselves and our family values. They were serious about keeping us out of trouble and teaching us self-respect.

You know what? We never got mixed up with drugs, which was a huge deal back then.

Looking back, it's incredible to think that I went from growing up in the projects to portraying life in the projects on television. It just goes to show that your beginnings don't dictate your future.

Cinderella in the Ghetto: The Road to Thelma

My brother, Gregory, once told me I was born to play Thelma, and since he has been with me throughout my life, he knows me best. Reflecting on my childhood, I've given a lot of thought to his words. Unlike Cinderella, I had two loving and protective parents. From an early age, I always knew I wanted to make a difference. By the time I was twelve, it was my dream to become a doctor of psychology.

On the subway, I used to observe people and wonder how the mind works and why people behave the way they do. This fascination continues to intrigue me even today. Sometimes, after my subway rides, I would mimic someone I had been watching. I was fortunate to study acting at the Center for Art & Culture of Bedford-Stuyvesant during high school, where I won a scholarship to attend classes every Monday night for a year. This experience broadened my understanding of acting and taught me how to study and break down a character's thought process. I enjoyed examining my characters' mindsets. Graduating high school and choosing a college was quite an experience, ultimately leading me to apply to Hunter College in New York City to study psychology.

Mom suggested I apply to the acting program at The Juilliard School of Music after she had a feeling about it during her subway ride home from work. I agreed, so she hired a Shakespearean actor to teach me Shakespearian and contemporary monologues, both required for the audition. I felt well-prepared, and the audition went smoothly. By the end, I was calm and satisfied with my performance.

I auditioned at the end of June, but I still had not heard from Juilliard by the end of August. I needed to know whether they had accepted me, as I would have to enroll at Hunter College if I hadn't. Previously, I auditioned for Juilliard as a ballerina, but they rejected me because I identified as a modern jazz dancer rather than a ballerina. I was nervous about how this audition would turn out.

I called Juilliard, and the woman who answered asked if I had received my acceptance letter. When I said no, she put me on hold to check. Those few minutes felt like the longest minutes of my life. When she returned to the phone and said, "Yes, you are accepted," those were the most wonderful words I had ever heard! I was ecstatic to be accepted into one of the most prestigious performing arts schools in the world. I immediately called my mother to share the good news, and she was so excited for me. On my way home, I was walking on cloud nine. I didn't enter Juilliard on a scholarship; my parents covered my tuition. Knowing that was a challenge for them, they made it work. I was beginning my second year at Juilliard when I landed the role of Thelma Evans, the first Black female teenager on television.

That summer brought two incredible opportunities: competing in the Miss Teenage Black America Pageant and landing the role of Thelma. It all began the year before when Mom, inspired by a vision, approached Hal Jackson, the head of the pageant, about including teenagers in the Miss Black America Pageant. He embraced her idea, leading to the launch of the Teenage Miss Black America Pageant the following summer. Excited about the opportunity, I begged Mom to let me participate. However, the financial reality tempered my reality—the costs of gowns, bathing suits, dresses, and shoes, a series of expenses to manage.

Undaunted, my family and I embarked on a weekly pilgrimage from Brooklyn to Manhattan, taking the subway every Sunday for pageant training in Central Park. This routine became a cherished part of our summer. The journey took an hour from home to the studio, where I would spend four hours of rehearsal.

On the day of the pageant, self-doubt gripped me as I stared at my reflection in the mirror and questioned my worthiness. "I've never won before. Why would today be any different?" When my mom called out for me to get ready, my decision not to participate solidified. "Mom, I'm not going," I declared, my attitude stubbornly defiant.

Her insistence only intensified my slow-as-molasses pace in getting dressed, driven by a rebellious spirit. On the subway ride, a cloud of resentment hung over us. Seated far from Mom, I plotted a petty revenge. Ever the actress, I feigned an asthma attack, strategically wheezing to amplify the drama. Triumphantly, I thought I had found my escape route.

Yet Mom's resilience remained unyielding. A detour to a nearby drugstore for Primatene® MIST became my reality check.

With a determined gaze, she declared, "BernNadette, you're going to take it and get up on that stage."

Confronted with Mom's strong resolve, I knew I couldn't back down. Gathering my courage, I pushed aside my doubts and stepped onto the stage, showing that the hardest struggles often happen inside us.

At the pageant, Kuno Spunholz, a talent manager, approached Mom and said, "We're doing a new TV show, and we're looking for a young lady to play the daughter in the show. It looks like your daughter would be great." He took a business card from his pocket. "Here, take my card and bring your daughter to the auditions at CBS Studios tomorrow."

Kuno was such a positive and lovely man—always so encouraging. He radiated warmth and confidence in my potential even during those early stages. His belief in me made a world of difference.

I came in as the first runner-up in the pageant, and I was grateful for the experience. I won a beautiful trophy, which I gave it to Mom because she was the real winner. The pageant not only led me to *Good Times*, but it also taught me a big life lesson: when God is getting ready to do something big in your life, negative thoughts can try to hold you back and make you doubt, potentially causing you to miss out on what God has in store for you. I'm grateful to have had a mother with faith strong enough to believe in me when I needed it the most. I always say, "Don't let fear stop you from walking into your destiny," because that Sunday, only fear tried to make me doubt and miss the pageant.

My destiny was to be Thelma on *Good Times*.

I will never forget the moment I found out I got the part of Thelma Evans. It was around 4:00 p.m., and I had just come home from the store. Mom was sitting on the couch with her legs crossed—something she rarely did. I looked into her eyes, and right away, knew something special had happened.

She looked at me and said, "You've got it. You're Thelma."

This was right around Christmas time, so I called it a Christmas present from heaven. Kuno was one of the first to celebrate with me, sending an enormous bouquet of gorgeous poinsettias and a stunning brown leather travel bag. His thoughtful gesture showed how genuinely happy he was for me. In that moment, we both shared the joy of what was to come, and it's a memory that remains close to my heart.

That day on the subway, I believe God had told Mom that I was to go to Juilliard to prepare for this upcoming opportunity. However, it wasn't quite like that. Mom thought I should try acting because I had been studying it for a year at a community theater in Bedford-Stuyvesant, and she believed I had real talent. Before that, around age twelve, I had taken dance classes with Bernice Johnson, the best and most exclusive snootiest dance instructor in town.

Despite my lack of enthusiasm, Mom insisted that I go to Ms. Johnson's dance studio, which was located about an hour away on Long Island, because it was the best. So, off I went. Also, I was auditioning for the Performing Arts High School nearby, a specialized school where students received rigorous training in music, dance, theater, and visual arts alongside academics. I had auditioned the year before and didn't make it. All of Ms. Johnson's students had gotten in, so I asked her for advice on what to do for my next audition. She suggested tap dancing. I practiced hard, learned a tap routine, and performed it at my audition—only to be rejected again!

Naturally, I felt disappointed, so I asked Ms. Johnson why I didn't get accepted. She said, "Because they don't accept tap dancers." What? She was the one who told me to tap dance! I was confused and frustrated. I knew I was a good dancer. My former dance instructor, Ms. Sloane, had told me so. This was one of those times I had to take some hits before landing a big win.

As fate would have it, when I was on my way to Los Angeles to play Thelma, I saw Ms. Johnson on the plane. We were both seated in first class.

Ms. Johnson saw me. "Hello, BernNadette. Where are you going?"

"To LA to do the pilot for a TV show."

"Oh, okay. What have you been up to?"

"I've been at Juilliard for the last eighteen months." I smiled.

"Where?" The look on her face showed her astonishment.

"I go to Juilliard."

"Oh, for dance?"

"No. Acting."

"I see…"

Although the Performing Arts High School didn't accept me like Ms. Johnson's other students, I made it into Juilliard, and they didn't. It just goes to show that your path to success may not look like everyone else's, and you may face disappointments along the way. However, the key is to keep going!

CHAPTER 2

Let the Good Times Roll

First Impressions

I moved from New York to California and lived alone for the first time in a studio apartment. Lonely and scared, I spent many nights on the phone with Mom. Back then, phones were attached to the wall, and long-distance calls between California and New York were not cheap! After that first year, my brother, Gregory, who is a year younger than me, moved out to California and in with me.

The significant life change was mind-blowing, but I was ready for the adventure. Hollywood had nothing on Brownsville; there were no surprises when it came to drugs or wild parties. I had already seen a lot of things in Brownsville, so I was not overwhelmed.

People often ask, "How come you never got caught up by Hollywood? You're still the same person you were before. Hollywood never changed you." My answer remains the same:

"Hollywood is just another place in the world, and I will remain the person I have always been no matter where I live." I am forever grateful to Mom and Dad for raising me that way.

Juilliard had prepared me to embody Thelma's character. I accepted that my life would be different since I was on a TV show that allowed me to do exactly what I had been studying at school—it was a dream come true. I had goals to achieve and stayed focused on them for my parents. I never wanted to disappoint them, and I didn't. I was on a mission, knowing my family depended on me. This responsibility never left my mind. I felt committed to helping Mom and Dad get out of the projects and ensuring that my siblings got an excellent education to achieve their goals. By the grace of God, this is what happened, and I was proud to contribute.

Our home base was CBS Studios on Beverly Boulevard in Los Angeles, California. Fridays began with a table read in the rehearsal hall from 10:00 a.m. to noon. Picture this: producers, writers, and actors gathered around a long table with scripts in hand, preparing for the upcoming episode. This was our chance to breathe life into the script and discuss any necessary tweaks. If significant revisions were required, the updated scripts would be sent to us at home by evening. Over the weekend, we dove into our lines, gearing up for Monday's rehearsals.

Director Herb Kent guided us through our paces, mapping out our movements on set. By Tuesday, they expected us to have our lines and blocking memorized. Rehearsals took up our whole day, concluding with an evening run-through for feedback from producers, writers, and wardrobe.

On Wednesday, we'd transitioned to the soundstage, where the set awaited us. We continued rehearsals as we fine-tuned our performances for the cameras and boom operators. Thursday marked tape day, the pinnacle of our week's efforts. With hair and makeup done, we ran through the show one last time before filming our first performance in front of a live studio audience of two hundred fifty people. After a quick dinner break, we'd return for our second show, repeating the process. The final cut of the episode seamlessly blended footage from both performances, creating the polished product that graced screens each week. It was awe-inspiring how they erected the set on Tuesday nights and dismantled it every Friday morning—a routine faithfully repeated week after week. Thus, the cycle began anew, with Friday's table read, signaling the start of another week of rehearsals and filming.

Memorizing my lines was easy. At Juilliard, I learned to tape-record my lines and listen to them repeatedly until they became ingrained in my subconscious. No, we didn't cheat! None of us hid our lines in case we forgot. Esther Rolle and John Amos influenced my acting greatly. Watching them was a valuable experience because they were both professional and always willing to teach us how to conduct ourselves on set.

Developing Thelma

The job requirements for being on a hit show include adapting to the pros and cons of both the role and the Hollywood lifestyle. Punctuality is crucial, which means being on time for work and leaving your personal life outside the rehearsal hall. Maintaining a pleasant and professional attitude, being easy to work with, getting along with your costars, and knowing all your lines are essential. As the show gained popularity, more and more people recognized us, and that fame could be both exciting and overwhelming.

Unlike real life, acting provides a regulated space where everything is orchestrated to produce a specific result. As an actress, I went through experiences similar to anyone else. If your character becomes popular, your life changes, and you must deal with the challenges of being recognized. Your privacy often becomes the price of fame, but it can be worthwhile if you can manage this aspect of being an actor or actress.

One memorable experience occurred when J.J., Michael, and I had our first appearance at a mall in California. I saw the crowd approaching the outdoor stage from the limousine and initially thought they were there for another star. To my surprise, they were there for us! That was when I truly understood what it felt like to be famous. I remember giving my first autograph. Jimmie and I went to the farmer's market next to CBS for lunch. While ordering, a woman approached us and asked for our autographs. She went to Jimmie first, and he signed his name. When she approached me, I not only signed but also wrote an inspirational message.

Jimmie said, "Don't write a book. Just sign your name."

That was how I learned how to give my fans a proper autograph.

Six months into *Good Times*, I felt my character's development had stagnated. I delivered the same lines—"Hi, Ma. Hi, Daddy," "Shut up, J.J.—and then retreated to the bathroom. Frustrated with the lack of growth, I confided in Esther, expressing my boredom and belief that I could bring more depth to the character. Esther, ever supportive, reassured me she would address it.

At the next rehearsal, a new script arrived, but my lines remained unchanged. However, true to her word, Esther seized the opportunity during the table read to advocate for me.

In front of producers and writers, she boldly asked, "Are you ashamed of my daughter?"

Stunned, they replied, "No."

"J.J. has a lot to say. Michael has a lot to say. My daughter has a lot to say, too. She deserves a voice like my sons."

The producers agreed.

Esther instructed me, "You go tell them who Thelma is."

Thelma was not a stereotypical character because I helped develop her. It is a rarity to shape your character in the acting world; you need time and space for that process. I am forever grateful for Esther's support, which allowed me to bring Thelma to life and give the first Black teenage girl on television a voice. I modeled my character after myself—she was the girl from the projects, just like me, except I'm a Capricorn and I made Thelma a Gemini. I recognized Thelma was a middle child and the only girl, so I ensured her behavior and attitudes reflected that. While Thelma was more optimistic and outgoing than I am, I drew inspiration from the script, classes from Juilliard, and books I read on the bus as a young girl. My childhood prepared me to act long before my first acting class.

It also takes time to study your lines and understand your character's direction. Once you have developed your character and feel confident in your lines and understanding, you're ready to explore different aspects of the role. That was how I approached playing Thelma.

Esther Rolle: A Motherly Force On and Off the Good Times Set

Born on November 8, 1920, Esther Rolle's remarkable career was characterized by versatility, activism, and a commitment to authentic storytelling. Before capturing our hearts as Florida Evans, Esther paved her path to stardom through her involvement with the Negro Ensemble Company.

Esther's theatrical roots deepened within this pioneering group, dedicated to showcasing African American talent and stories. Through her work with the Ensemble, Esther honed her craft, contributing to groundbreaking productions that addressed critical social issues and celebrated the richness of African American culture. Her nuanced performances and fearlessness in tackling challenging topics made her an invaluable asset to our show and a national treasure.

Norman Lear first recognized Esther Rolle's exceptional talent. A perceptive and forward-thinking creator of *Maude*, Lear cast her as the maid, appreciating her ability to bring depth and authenticity to her characters. This pivotal moment in her career led Lear to envision Esther as the lead in her own series, which eventually became *Good Times*. Initially proposing a narrative about a single mother with three children, Lear faced Esther's unwavering commitment to genuine representation.

Drawing from her upbringing, where both parents played active roles, Esther insisted her character have a husband and father to model a positive depiction of Black family life. She shaped the narrative of *Good Times* by breaking stereotypes and highlighting the involvement of Black men in their families. Her vision added depth to her character as my on-screen mom and contributed to reshaping the portrayal of African American families on television.

I am reminded of and struck by the depth of Esther's journey—a journey marked by artistic excellence, activism, and a commitment to fostering a more inclusive narrative for future generations. She was a phenomenal actress who played a pivotal role as my on-screen mother, creating a bond that transcended scripted lines.

I vividly remember the first time I walked into the rehearsal hall and saw her there—Ms. Rolle, exuding grace and warmth. I introduced myself as BernNadette, and from that moment on, our connection blossomed. She welcomed me with open arms, and our on-screen relationship evolved into a genuine mother-daughter dynamic.

This dynamic manifested in many ways, including problem-solving. One day during rehearsal, a secretary from Norman's office approached me to explain that my name was too long to fit into the credits on the screen. Unsure what that meant, I learned they wanted me to shorten my name.

My last name is Stanislaus, so when the issue came up, I went over to Ms. Rolle, whom I called Mom, and asked, "Mom, where should I cut my name off to shorten it?"

Esther looked at my name and said, "Cut it right here," and that's how I became BernNadette Stanis. From that day on, my name changed professionally.

I called my dad back in Brooklyn and said, "Dad, from now on, when you see my name on the credits, it will be Stanis instead of Stanislaus."

Dad said, "Okay, Stanis, Stanislaus, it's okay." His acceptance put me at ease.

So, Esther Rolle gave me my professional last name.

While we're on the topic of my name, here's a fan fact: I changed the spelling of my name from Bernadette to BernNadette as part of a 1970s trend of personal and creative expression. I still spell it that way today.

I always felt safe with Esther during the show. She was not just a co-star but a fierce advocate for all of us. Living just around the corner from me, she took it upon herself to be my daily chauffeur to work since I didn't drive then. We agreed I would be downstairs at 9:00 a.m. sharp. It became a valuable lesson in punctuality.

Each morning, though, I arrived later and later. One day, Esther warned me that if I were late again, she would leave without me. I chuckled, not believing she would actually do

BernNadette and Esther Rolle share chuckle while reading Good Times script. The elder actress has taken the younger one under her show biz wing.

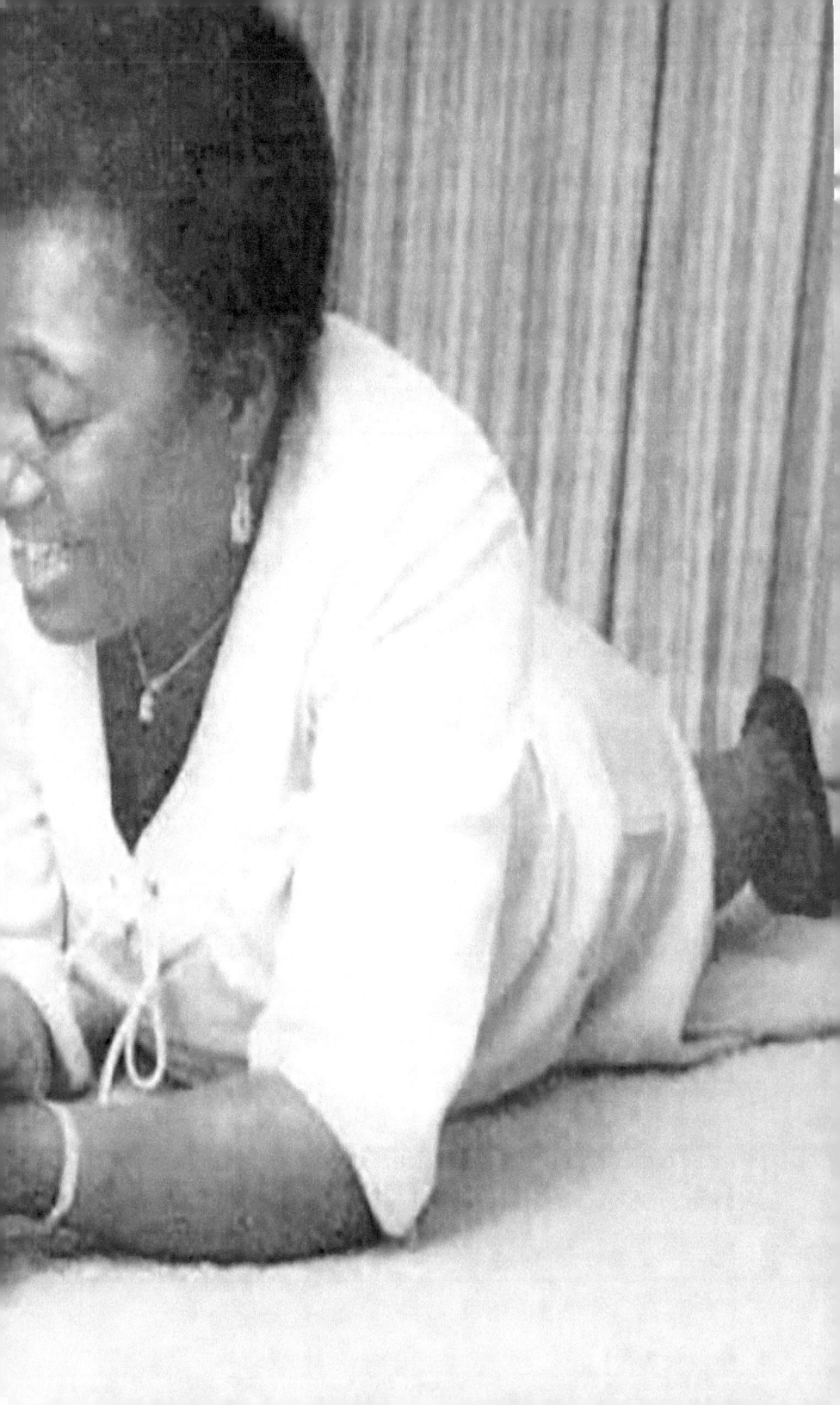

it. The next morning, as fate would have it, I was late again. I headed downstairs, only to discover that her car was missing. She was *definitely* not waiting for me. True to her word, she had indeed left.

In those days, without taxi apps, getting a ride wasn't easy, and it took me hours to get to work. When I finally walked into the rehearsal hall at 1:00 p.m., there was Esther with that all-knowing I-told-you-so look. I couldn't even be mad—I respected her for being a woman of her word. Esther wasn't just a co-star; she was a mentor, teaching me life lessons beyond the script.

Eventually, I got my driver's license. I had a driving instructor who would call me every morning at 6:30 a.m. sharp, addressing me as "Miss Nadette" and asking if I was ready for my lesson. I'd scramble out of bed, assuring him I'd be downstairs in ten minutes. This routine ritual went on for months until test day finally arrived.

However, luck seemed to be against me that day—it seemed like every street was under construction, and my nerves got the best of me. The driving examiner eventually stopped the test and told me, "Pull over and park, and come back when you learn how to drive." Ouch! Determined not to give up, I rented a car with a friend's help and spent the entire weekend driving around, practicing. When Monday came, I took the test again—I passed with flying colors.

Lifelong Friends

After *Good Times*, I stayed close to Esther Rolle. She often updated me on her work—performing in various shows and movies, and giving speeches at schools. Her one-woman show about Harriet Tubman took her across the country. She also reminisced about the outfits made by Adella Farmar, who also styled the *Good Times* cast, and Billy, who managed her hair. The bond we formed on the show continued even after production ended. We traveled together, dined out, and spent quality time at each other's homes.

As time when on, Esther began experiencing health issues. My two-year-old daughter, Brittany, and I accompanied her to doctor's appointments every Tuesday. I still remember her first impression of Brittany. She exclaimed, "Oh, Bern, she's so pretty!"

Our routine was simple: I would visit Esther's house around 11:00 a.m., and then drive her to her appointment, which typically lasted from 1:00 to 4:00 p.m. On the way home, Esther always suggested grabbing a bite to eat. I would remind her of her dietary restrictions, but she insisted on indulging in comfort food. At first, I didn't fully understand why, but as her health declined, I realized this was her way of embracing life's little joys. So, we enjoyed soul food—fried chicken, mashed potatoes, corn on the cob, sweet tea—and Esther always got a sweet potato pie to go.

On that last Tuesday, I sat down with Esther and shared my upcoming plans: a stage play in the Virgin Islands that required me to leave by Thursday. I promised to return on Monday to take her to her next appointment. I also mentioned that I planned to cook a hearty pot of vegetables for her, as I felt she needed more nutritious meals.

As I spoke, Esther took my hand and said, "I want to thank you, Bern, for being such a great daughter to me. Take care of Brittany."

Her words touched me deeply, and I said, "I really love you, Mom."

As we walked to her door, Brittany spotted a ladybug on one of Esther's bushes. Excitedly, she picked it up and insisted we give it to Esther as a gift.

Esther smiled and said, "Thank you, Brittany. I will keep it forever."

After completing the play, I returned home on Monday, only to wake up the next day to the devastating news of Esther's passing on November 17, 1998. Reflecting on our last moments together, I realized the significance of her words and Brittany's simple gesture. It was our way of saying goodbye to a remarkable woman who meant the world to us. I'm forever grateful for the opportunity to have been by her side during her final days, which brought a sense of closure to a bond that will always hold a special place in my heart.

Damn, Damn, Damn!

I frequently get asked why Florida exclaimed, "Damn, damn, damn!" at the conclusion of the episode about James' death. Esther coined this phrase, with each "damn" carrying its own unique significance. The first damn said, "I hate to lose John as a castmate." The second damn was disappointment that the show was going to be minus a father figure after how hard Esther fought for the Evans to be a two-parent family. Yet, there it was, again, the Black home without a father figure. The third damn was realizing she would have to navigate the show alone. These realizations were difficult and hurtful for her at the same time.

Esther was a woman of principle and activism. She passionately advocated for positive and realistic portrayals of African American characters in the media to combat racial stereotypes. Making a broad-scale impact was her goal, which was evident in her dedication to social issues. She lived her life with resilience and grace. Her experiences shaped her into the strong, principled woman we all admired. Esther's personal and professional lives intertwined, leaving a lasting legacy. Those of us who had the privilege of working with her continue to pay her vibrant influence forward to future generations.

CHAPTER 3

Kings of the Set: My Good Times Costars

John Amos

Though only thirty-four when *Good Times* began (compared to Esther, who was fifty-four), John Amos wasn't just a talented actor but a guiding presence both on and off the set. His portrayal of James Evans, my strong, principled father figure, was more than just a role; it reflected his deeply held values. Like Esther, John drew from his childhood experiences, particularly the importance of fatherhood in the Black community. His commitment to authenticity and representation resonated deeply with us, fostering a sense of solidarity and purpose on set. Beyond his acting skills, John's mentorship left a lasting impact. As a newcomer to the industry, I was fortunate to receive invaluable advice from him about maneuvering the complexities of Hollywood. He warned me about the industry's potential pitfalls and the

importance of guarding oneself against exploitation—lessons I carried throughout my career.

John's love for horses and ranches revealed another side of his multifaceted personality. He welcomed us into his world, inviting us to share in his passions. Spending time with John was always a warm and camaraderie-filled experience, whether it was relaxing by the pool, playing guitars and sharing stories, or exploring his expansive ranch.

As a co-star, I witnessed firsthand John's dedication to his role as a father figure, both on and off the screen, especially with his children: K.C. and Shannon. His interactions with them mirrored the warmth and affection he brought to his portrayal of my TV dad, reinforcing the authenticity of his performance. John Amos was like a real dad to us on the set. He treated me like his real daughter and gave me the nickname "Baby Girl." When I think of John, I picture him reading—he amazed me by reading thick books weekly. He was incredibly well-read.

At my first dinner at a CBS Hollywood Gala, I sat at the *Good Times* table to John's right. I was extremely excited to be surrounded by stars I had grown up watching on television and in the movies. I had heard that Billy Dee Williams would be attending and as a true fan—especially after seeing him in *Bryan's Song*—I was excited to meet him and get an autograph. I had even prepared by tucking a small piece of decorative paper and a pen into my purse.

Good Times, Ain't We Lucky We Got 'Em:
Memoir of an American Sweetheart

When Billy Dee Williams finally entered with his son, I watched closely as he made his way to the table right in front of us. I had a plan: once he reached a certain spot, I would approach him for the autograph. As he neared that perfect moment, I got up from my seat, grabbed my purse, and prepared to make my move. However, just as I was halfway up, I felt a hand grab my arm.

It was John. He asked, "Where are you going?" I believe he knew because it was plain to see.

I was fanning out just a little, so I said, "I am going to get his autograph."

"Bern, sit down. You can't do that."

"Why?"

"You are one of them now."

He meant I was a star, too, and stars don't ask for autographs, no matter how big of a fan they are. I sat down, but I was so disappointed. My icon was sitting right there in front of me, and I couldn't get the autograph I had dreamed of. It was a reality check—a moment when I realized I was now part of Hollywood's celebrity society, and with that came a new set of expectations. That was just the beginning of the sacrifices I would have to make.

It took me forty years to get Billy Dee Williams' autograph at Comic-Con in San Diego. Yes, I stood in line to get it, and no one stopped me this time.

Everyone knew John had differing opinions from the show's writers and producers. Professionally, this didn't affect me much since I wasn't privy to the details. I was busy being Thelma and a young woman learning to navigate a new career and the nuances of fame.

However, I think an external influence may have escalated the situation. *Ebony* magazine approached our cast for an interview, and we agreed. When the article was published in the September 1975 issue, it painted a very negative picture. Titled "Bad Times on the *Good Times* Set," it focused on alleged infighting between the cast and producers, overlooking the positive impact the show was having. While some conflicts existed, as they do in any workplace, *Ebony* took advantage of those talking points and made them the centerpiece of the article. This was unfortunate for our cast and fans because history has shown the tremendous positive impact our show had on viewers, opening doors for future Black television shows.

At the next table read, we gathered around, as usual, and went through the script. Norman Lear was there, and after we finished, he set his script aside and placed the *Ebony* article on the table. He wasn't angry, but rather disappointed and heartbroken. The *Good Times* set felt like a family, and this incident came across as a betrayal. Until that moment, I had not realized that Norman was unaware of the interview, and the tension it caused visibly saddened him. It was like that feeling you get when your parents are fighting, and you just want everything to be okay again. In my opinion, this contributed to the breakdown of the show.

Good Times, Ain't We Lucky We Got 'Em:
Memoir of an American Sweetheart

In a 2016 documentary about Norman Lear's life, John talked about the friction he had with the producers and writers, sharing that he took his role as James Evans very seriously and wanted to portray it right. Norman said, "John, don't take this quite so seriously. You have a wonderful role. Enjoy it." John, however, explained, "I was taking it extremely personally, to the point that the writers got tired of their lives being threatened over jokes and scripts and punch lines. My thing was 'Take the crap out, or let's fight'" (*Norman Lear: Just Another Version of You*, 00:51:43-00:52:06).

When John left the show, I was confused—it was a complete shock. I didn't even know he was gone until I read the script. However, John and I have stayed close over the years. I remember when my baby daughter, Brittany, and I visited him in San Diego. We took a lovely train ride from Los Angeles, and when we arrived, John met us at the station and took us to where he kept his boat. We enjoyed a wonderful lunch that he cooked for us, and we spent the afternoon together. John was very impressed with Brittany, saying she was such a bright child, and he just fell in love with her. She adored him, too. It was a beautiful day—we even played a game of chess. I played a good game, but John won. Later that afternoon, he drove us back to the train station so Brittany and I could return to Los Angeles.

When John's mother passed away, he called and asked if I would attend her funeral. Of course, I wanted to support him, so I went. At the service, John shared a cute story about his childhood. He said that one Friday afternoon he came home from kindergarten. He said, "Mom, I want my nose to be straight instead of the way it is."

His mom said, "Okay. You can put this clothespin on your nose for the weekend, and Monday, when you go back to school, your nose will be straight."

So, all weekend, John wore a clothespin on his nose, and on Monday, when he was getting ready for school, he took it off to see if his nose had gotten straight. John's nose remained the same.

He said, "Look, Mom. It didn't change."

His mom said, "That is your nose, John, and it's not going to change."

John realized he had to learn to love his nose. I believe he did learn to love his nose because it had never been a problem, and it certainly never stopped him from being a success.

Even after *Good Times* ended, John's star continued to shine brightly in the entertainment industry. From his ventures in film to his successful stage productions, including the renowned *Hayley's Comet*, John's talent and versatility knew no bounds. I, and countless others, will always remember John Amos with admiration and affection. His portrayal of James Evans remains iconic—a symbol of fatherhood, resilience, and unwavering principles. In a world of fleeting fame and shifting values, John's steadfast commitment to his beliefs serves as a beacon of inspiration for future generations.

Unfortunately, while writing this book, John passed away on August 15, 2024.

Jimmie Walker

Jimmie Walker, whom we simply called Jimmie on set, was the heart and soul of *Good Times*. Even before landing his role on the show, he was already an accomplished stand-up comedian. Playing the role of my big brother J.J., he brought more than just laughs to our TV family. Jimmie had an incredible ability to light up a room with his energy and humor. You couldn't help but smile when Jimmie was around—his infectious laugh could lift anyone's spirits, whether we were filming or just hanging out during breaks.

Good Times, Ain't We Lucky We Got 'Em: Memoir of an American Sweetheart

As J.J., he brought his character to life with vibrant paintings and his signature bright smile, making the whole room lighter with his presence.

Off-camera, Jimmie was—and still is—family. His natural charm and warmth made him a joy to be around. We'd share stories and joke around, and he always had a new joke or impersonation to entertain us. It might surprise many to learn that Jimmie, in real life, is quite different from his flamboyant and extroverted TV character, J.J. While J.J. is his alter ego, the real Jimmie is calm, quiet, and has a wonderful sense of humor.

I first encountered Jimmie Walker during my audition for *Good Times* at CBS Studios. It was a nerve-racking experience, as it was my first audition for a television show. Aspiring actresses packed the room, including a couple of familiar faces like Beverly Johnson and Debbie Allen. The energy was electric, filled with anticipation.

As I waited, I recalled my father's reassuring words: "What's for you is for you, and no one can take it from you." His advice steadied my nerves until they called my name. I walked into the audition room and immediately noticed Norman Lear and Jimmie Walker, both wearing their signature hats they always wore during auditions—Norman's white canvas pork-pie hat and Jimmie's J.J.'s denim bucket hat. Norman, seated behind a desk, handed me a script to read, but I hesitated because the dialogue didn't feel authentic for a teenage girl from the projects. Drawing on my own experiences growing up, I asked if I could improvise. Norman gave me a skeptical look but allowed it. Jimmie and I improvised a playful argument about cleaning the house, which drew laughter from Norman.

I remember saying something like, "J.J., you better help me clean up this house before Mama gets home from work."

Jimmie retorted, "No, I'm not cleaning up anything."

"Yes, you are!" I playfully swatted his shoulder. "You can at least take out the garbage."

After the audition, I thanked them and left, unsure of what would happen. More than a month passed with no word, and then I suddenly got the call to fly to California for a week. I joined three other girls: Chip Fields (Kim Fields' mother), Tamu Blackwell, who starred in *Claudine* alongside Diahann Carroll, and Stephanie, a local Californian actress.

The studio arranged for me to stay at a hotel called The Farmer's Daughter, which is now Short Stories Hotel Los Angeles, conveniently located across the street from CBS Studios. The next day, we gathered at the studio and met on the soundstage where the *Good Times* living room set—complete with J.J. perched on it—awaited us. This was my second encounter with Jimmie Walker.

We received another script that we had to learn. Eventually, they called us to audition with Jimmie. It felt like the audition process stretched for hours as we had to perform the script multiple times alongside Jimmie. This routine continued daily for a week, with different scenes and scripts each day.

After that intense week, I was returning to Brooklyn, New York. While waiting at the airport, surprisingly, my name came over the loudspeaker, instructing me to go to the information desk. There, I learned that CBS Studios had called and wanted me to stay in California for another week. A driver picked me up and took me back to The Farmer's Daughter.

The following day, we returned to CBS Studios. Once again, we went through auditions with Jimmie, working on various scenes and scripts. During those auditions, I truly got to know Jimmie. This experience marked the beginning of a journey that would change my life, introducing me not only to the world of television but also to the warmth and talent of Jimmie, whose presence and humor made those days unforgettable.

When we started the show and began rehearsals, Jimmie was always punctual, but notably reserved. I understood why—he spent evenings at the Comedy Store on Sunset Boulevard in Hollywood, perfecting his material. Alongside his personal team of writers who contributed to *Good Times*, he prepared for his stand-up shows, which took him nationwide on weekends. His writers included Jay Leno, Byron Allen, David Letterman, David Brenner, and even Freddie Prinze, all of whom he helped launch into their own successful careers.

Jimmie later played a key role in bringing Shirley Hemphill onto *Good Times*, while also supporting her on her show, *What's Happening!*

Having known her from their shared nights at the Comedy Store, where she performed nightly, I could understand why Jimmie seemed tired in the mornings, surrounded by his comedian friends. Despite his quiet demeanor during rehearsals, Jimmie always delivered his lines flawlessly. What impressed me most about Jimmie was his ability to memorize all his lines without missing a beat. Initially, I thought his writers were the key to his success, but I soon realized it was simply his vast experience as a seasoned comedian, accustomed to handling large volumes of material. That made delivering lines on *Good Times* seem effortless for him.

Dyn-O-Mite!

The phrase "Dyn-O-Mite" was born almost accidentally during a rehearsal. Jimmie Walker casually tossed it out while delivering a line. The guest director, John Rich, a friend of Norman Lear's, became captivated and exclaimed, "I love that dynamite thing!" He urged Jimmie to emphasize it, insisting, "That's what we need—you've got to do it like that."

John Rich then jumped up and took center stage. He clapped his hands, grinned widely, and exaggerated the word with flair, saying, "Put your teeth into it—don't just say 'dynamite' like it's any other word. Say it big, with the smile, with everything!"

Jimmie, initially skeptical, protested, "Come on, nobody's going to go for that," but Rich insisted, and after a few takes, it exploded—figuratively and literally—into the show's fabric.

Not everyone was on board, though. Norman famously disliked it, calling it "the stupidest thing" he'd ever seen. However, John Rich fought for the catchphrase and eventually reached a compromise. Jimmie would say "Dyn-O-Mite" only once per episode, turning it into a moment that the audience eagerly awaited.

To this day, Jimmie can't escape the phrase. At book signings and events, fans still call him "Kid Dyn-O-Mite" and beg him to say it. As Jimmie loves to joke, "The phrase has been 'retired to the Smithsonian.'"

During rehearsals on set, Jimmie was speaking between takes, though I can't recall the specific topic of conversation.

Big Brother

Our bond as brother and sister was immediate and comfortable from the start. One day, Jimmie asked me about a girl he had recently met. He seemed quite taken with her and wanted my advice on how to impress her. When I asked if he liked her a lot, he admitted he did. I suggested he consider getting her something nice, like a piece of jewelry.

During a lunch break at the studio, Jimmie followed my suggestion. He went to the farmer's market next to CBS Studios, and when he returned, he proudly showed me a large turquoise necklace adorned with thick silver accents. I couldn't resist teasing him, asking if he was dating a giant, given the size of the necklace. Gently, I encouraged him to choose something more elegant and subtle, like a beautiful necklace with a delicate diamond pendant.

Taking my advice to heart, Jimmie exchanged the turquoise necklace for a stunning piece made of white gold, accentuated with a sparkling diamond pendant. It was truly exquisite—something any woman would cherish. To this day, Jimmie has a great eye for selecting beautiful jewelry for the special women in his life.

Beyond his knack for gift-giving, Jimmie had a deep passion for sports. Even while we were filming the show, he had connections with many professional athletes. He would often excitedly tell me about these athletes and offer to introduce me to them. However, sports were never my thing,

so I never took him up on his generous offers. Looking back, I can't help but think about what I missed out on.

On tape days, every Thursday, Jimmie greeted me with an abundance of flowers from these athletes. He still loves to tell the story of intercepting the delivery guy to make sure the flowers made it to my dressing room while sneaking a few for himself to give to his dates.

About three months into our show, when options for going out were limited and company was scarce, I asked Jimmie if I could join him one evening at the Comedy Store. After persistent nudging and hints, he finally relented, telling me to be ready by 9:00 p.m.

When I came down from my apartment to meet him, I found three comedians in the car. I squeezed into the back seat with the two of them—David Brenner and Freddie Prinze—while Jay Leno occupied the front passenger seat. Throughout the ride and even at the Comedy Store, those comedians bantered non-stop, exchanging jokes and stories as if they were performing on stage right then and there. Despite my initial hopes that the chatter would die down, it never did. Once at the Comedy Store, each delivered their sets, and I watched in awe as they seamlessly transitioned from car banter to on-stage performance.

After *Good Times*, Jimmie's talent as a stand-up comedian and actor grew. He had a unique ability to connect with audiences, whether on stage or screen. His achievements in television and popular culture are undeniable. The world will forever remember Jimmie Walker as J.J., the character who, everywhere he went, brought laughter, love, and a bit of "Dyn-o-mite!" Jimmie and I stay in touch and see each other regularly.

Ralph Carter

My first encounter with Ralph Carter took place in the rehearsal hall around 11:00 a.m. on the first morning. Since he received tutoring on set, his schedule differed from ours. I was immediately struck by Ralph's strong presence. I had heard so much about his incredible performances in Broadway plays and musicals, particularly his role in the musical version of *A Raisin in the Sun*. It was fascinating to learn that Norman Lear had to negotiate a significant buyout of Ralph's Broadway contract, paying over $50,000—an astronomical amount in 1974. What amazed me even more was the coincidence that my biological brother, Talbert Kethrell Stanislaus, ended up replacing Ralph on Broadway. Landing the role of Thelma on *Good Times* and seeing my brother step into that big opportunity in New York City was, indeed, a great moment of pride for me.

Working with Ralph on set, I witnessed his professionalism and talent firsthand. Despite being only eleven, he approached his work with a level of discipline and skill far beyond his years. He was not only a great actor but also an impressive singer, always coming to set prepared and knowing his lines flawlessly.

Good Times, Ain't We Lucky We Got 'Em:
Memoir of an American Sweetheart

Mrs. Katherine Jackson, Janet Jackson, Lucille Carter (Ralph Carter's mom), and Janet's teacher, Mr. Mainer (back row)

Ralph already had built relationships with John Amos and Esther Rolle from their previous shows, which contributed to the warm and welcoming atmosphere on set. Getting to know Ralph Carter personally during *Good Times* was a privilege. His dedication to his craft and his kind personality left a lasting impression on me, making our shared experiences on the show even more meaningful.

Ralph Carter's mother, Lucille, was like a mother to everyone on set. She was the epitome of a solid homemaker. Every Sunday, Lucille would prepare a big dinner, and she always invited my brother, Gregory Kyle, and me to join her family for these meals. She was the best cook I've ever known.

Originally from South Carolina, she could prepare every dish imaginable and was also an exceptional baker, able to bake all kinds of cakes from scratch. Ralph and his siblings were truly lucky to have her as a mother.

Lucille also looked after other young entertainers and those just starting their journey to success. Her home was not only beautiful but also incredibly cozy. Some notable celebrities, like Debbie Allen—when she was a guest on *Good Times*—and Hall of Famer Earvin "Magic" Johnson, before his rise to fame, stayed at her home.

What I loved most about Lucille's house was the beautiful décor and the exquisite plants she had everywhere. Though she was a tiny lady, she was always well-dressed and simply adorable. It's no wonder Ralph turned out to be such an amazing young man. He and I have always been very close and supported each other throughout the years.

Today, Ralph is very active in New York City, where he lives. He mentors young artists and serves on the Board of Directors for the AUDELCO Awards, which recognizes and honors Black theatre and its artists in New York City. Ralph is also a prolific writer and reader and is the creator of the television series *Grandma's Hands*. His brilliant portrayal of Michael on *Good Times* truly reflects the person Ralph Carter is today.

CHAPTER 4

Familiar Faces

Ja'Net DuBois: Everyone's Favorite Neighbor

Ja'Net DuBois played Willona Woods, bringing her vivacious and compassionate character to life in a way that endeared her to audiences worldwide. Her portrayal earned her critical acclaim and solidified her status as a television icon. A seasoned performer, Ja'Net had entertained audiences since childhood, and her talents extended far beyond acting. As a soulful storyteller, she ventured into music, performing as a singer in various nighttime venues, enchanting listeners with her voice.

Ja'Net was also a devoted mother to her four children—Kesha, Provat, Rani, and Raj—whom she raised with love and care. Despite the demands of her career, she always prioritized her family, instilling in them values of resilience, creativity, and compassion.

Her talent amazed me daily. It was a privilege to witness her infectious energy and steadfast dedication to her craft. One day during a rehearsal, I noticed her sitting beside a tape recorder, deeply absorbed in her work. Curious, I approached her and asked what she was recording and writing. She explained that she was composing a theme song for Norman Lear's new show, *The Jeffersons*, intending to present it to him by lunchtime. Excited for her, I asked if I could hear it. She graciously agreed, and as the music filled the room, the dancer in me came alive.

At lunchtime, Ja'Net presented the song to Norman, and after lunch, she returned with a radiant smile, sharing the fantastic news—he loved it and planned to use it. It was a triumphant moment, and I felt grateful to have been a part of it. Her theme song, "Movin' on Up," became an iconic part of *The Jeffersons*, capturing the spirit of optimism and ambition that defined the show. Its infectious melody and uplifting lyrics earned it a permanent place in television history.

In addition to her musical talents, Ja'Net had a poetic soul. I vividly remember the heartfelt poem she wrote for me, capturing the essence of womanhood with grace and depth. Her ability to express emotions through verse left a lasting impression on me, revealing yet another facet of her creative brilliance.

According to Catchy Comedy, Ja'Net DuBois intuitively understood the essence of *The Jeffersons*' theme song before even seeing the show. "They asked me how I was able to write that song without ever seeing what the show was about. I didn't have to see it to know. I know what we're going to do when we get some money; we're going to move; move to the hills or somewhere," DuBois added. "The first thing we are going to do is move out—move on up. And that is what they did, right? We always do" (Catchy Comedy Staff, "Ja'Net DuBois Wrote, '*The Jeffersons*' Theme Song Without Seeing the Show,'" catchycomedy.com).

Ja'Net also mentioned being inspired by her mother, who had always told her to write about what she dreamed of doing for her mother. Since childhood, she had promised her mother she would move her from the West Side to the East Side one day. That song reflected her desire to make a better life for herself and her loved ones.

On set, Ja'Net radiated elegance, and her impeccable fashion sense added to her charm. I cherished the special moments we shared—whether it was receiving admiration during a book signing or simply enjoying each other's company between takes. She was not only talented but also stylish and graceful.

My last interaction with Ja'Net was at a book signing event. I was genuinely happy for her as she basked in compliments about her enduring beauty from fellow cast members. Amid the lively conversation, we shared a mirror, touching up our lipstick—a simple yet intimate moment that reminded me of the bond we shared both on and off the set. However, the joy was tinged with sadness, as the recent passing of Kobe Bryant weighed heavily on all of our hearts. The entire cast came together to honor his memory, unknowingly foreshadowing the sorrow that was yet to come.

The following day, as Ja'Net stepped out of her hotel room, she confided that she hadn't slept well the night before, her words carrying a sense of unease. We proceeded with our scheduled book signing, cherishing the time together as if we knew it would be our last. As we said our goodbyes, a strange premonition gripped me—I couldn't shake the feeling that it might be the last time I'd see her.

Sadly, my intuition proved true. Just two weeks later, on February 17, 2020, I received a call from Ja'Net's daughter with the heartbreaking news of her passing. Reflecting on our final moments together, I treasure the memories we made and mourn the loss of a dear friend and colleague. Ja'Net's presence, both on and off the screen, is deeply missed, but her legacy of talent, kindness, and friendship will endure forever.

Ja'Net DuBois was a beacon of inspiration throughout her life and career, breaking barriers and exceeding expectations with grace and determination. Her legacy as a trailblazer, a visionary artist, and a beloved mother and friend will resonate for generations, a lasting testament to the power of her spirit and creativity.

Ben Powers: Selecting My Husband

Working with Ben was a joy. He brought an effortless charm to rehearsals, often adding humor by using different voices and personas for his character. He made the entire process fun and easy. Ben's vibrant personality and talent made filming as husband and wife a delightful experience.

The Wedding

The wedding was a precious moment for me. My character, Thelma, was about to marry Keith Anderson, and the writers had a lot to consider. What direction should Thelma take? It was the 1970s, a time when women in their twenties often got married and started families, but societal norms were shifting.

Good Times, Ain't We Lucky We Got 'Em: Memoir of an American Sweetheart

Thelma was always breaking new ground, and I felt I was right there with her, pushing against society's expectations. Portraying a Black female on television, I was exploring uncharted territory myself. So, the question lingered: How could Thelma's storyline contribute to this evolving narrative for women?

There were debates: Should she get married or pursue her education? Why not both? That idea was groundbreaking at the time. Thelma, much like me, was forward-thinking. She wanted both marriage and an education, a departure from the old-fashioned mindset of my parents' generation. Thelma embodied the spirit of the 1970s, an era of change. By getting married and continuing her studies, she blazed a trail for women, a path many still follow today. I take immense pride in being part of that pioneering journey.

The wedding ceremony was magical, almost like a real-life event. Keith and I exchanged heartfelt vows, and Adella Farmar, our wardrobe mistress, provided an exquisite wedding gown, which was hers that she wore on her wedding day. It fitted like a dream—a delicate mix of lace and satin. To this day, reminiscing about the wedding fills me with joy. It was a moment frozen in time, representing Thelma's journey and our impact on television history.

There was also a deeper emotional layer behind the scenes. Esther Rolle returned to the set after being gone for a year. You might remember that after John Amos left,

Esther's character remarried and moved to Arizona. We were thrilled to have her back on set, and our joy translated to the characters, making the episode more authentic.

Our wedding episode was historic—it was the first African American wedding ever depicted on television. We knew it was monumental, but I don't think anyone realized how impactful it would become. Years later, fans still tell me how our wedding inspired them, with some even choosing our wedding song, "You and I" by Stevie Wonder, for their ceremonies. While Stevie didn't sing it on the show, Ralph Carter delivered a beautiful rendition. Hearing those stories warms my heart and reaffirms the importance of Thelma walking down the aisle. We contributed to a broader cultural shift, and that legacy endures.

The Vows

Thelma's
I take this vow to share with you that which God shall let me share. To give to you that which God shall let me give. To be one with you, for I love you and ask only that this love shall sustain itself for the rest of our lives.

Keith's
I take this vow to love you as I do now and will forever and pray there be no bounds to this love so that it may grow stronger and stronger in all the years that God shall give us together.

Janet Jackson: A Legend in the Making

Janet Jackson, my dear co-star on *Good Times*, was a ray of sunshine bursting onto the entertainment scene. Born on May 16, 1966, in Gary, Indiana, Janet's talent sparkled even as the youngest member of our cast, beginning her extraordinary journey in the entertainment world.

In our beloved sitcom, Janet brought the character of Penny Gordon Woods to life, effortlessly showcasing her natural acting ability at a young age. As her on-set sister, I had the joy of witnessing Janet's unwavering commitment and sheer talent firsthand. Her performance on *Good Times* was just the beginning, as she later ventured into the world of music and dance with limitless potential.

Beyond the scripted lines, Janet's warmth and infectious energy lit up the set every day. We shared laughter, faced challenges, and celebrated victories together, forming a bond that transcended our on-screen roles. Little did we know that Janet Jackson would become a global icon, making an indelible mark on the music industry.

Her voice was unmatched, her stage presence mesmerizing, and her music videos groundbreaking, capturing the hearts of audiences worldwide. I swell with pride reflecting on how my former co-star evolved into the influential and revolutionary artist she is today. Janet's influence is a testament to her exceptional talent and her profound impact on pop culture, inspiring countless artists and fans across generations.

Janet always felt like my little sister, and I cherished playing the big sister role to her on set. I recall the time her brothers came to see her perform. Michael, in his playful way, said to Janet, regarding me, "Oh, Janet, she kinda looks like you."

Michael Jackson often attended the tapings, cleverly disguised so no one, including the cast and audience, recognized him. Janet would confide in Adella Farmar, saying, "Oh, my brother Michael will be here tonight." Yet, his disguise kept him hidden in plain sight.

Janet's professionalism, even as a ten-year-old, was remarkable. She knew her lines perfectly and carried herself with quiet dedication. At the end of taping nights, Adella would visit her dressing room, which was always impeccably organized. Janet's outfit, socks, shoes, earrings, and bows were all neatly arranged, a testament to her meticulous nature. Seeing such dedication in someone so young was truly inspiring.

Twelve-year-old Gary Coleman made a guest appearance on *Good Times*, kick-starting his acting career. He was immediately smitten with Janet. One night, Janet hurried to me, clearly upset, and said, "Oh, Bern, can you please tell him to leave me alone?" Without hesitation, I went up to Gary, gently grabbed his arm, and told him firmly to back off. I think it startled him, but from that moment on, he kept his distance. A year later, he landed the role of Arnold on *Diff'rent Strokes*.

Over time, I developed a close friendship with the Jackson family. I have fond memories of our interactions. When my mother visited me in California, we would often visit Mrs. Katherine Jackson's house, enjoying games of Uno and Pictionary. I fondly remember one instance when Mrs. Jackson drew a perfect tuba during Pictionary. I recognized the instrument but couldn't remember its name, causing us to lose the game. Despite the outcome, the laughter and camaraderie we shared during those moments remain cherished memories.

Johnny Brown (Buffalo Butt)

Johnny Brown's presence on the show was incredibly impactful. As the lovable and charismatic building superintendent, Nathan Bookman, Johnny brought more heartfelt laughter to our television family, making his addition to the cast a wonderful enhancement.

When he first walked onto the set, he was a ball of sunshine quietly studying everything happening around him. He said I was the first to come over to him, say hello, smile warmly, and welcome him to the show. Working with Johnny was always a delight; he entertained us during rehearsals with captivating stories from his show business career and impressive John Wayne impressions. I particularly enjoyed listening to the stories about him and Sammy Davis, Jr., with whom he worked on many shows, like *Golden Boy*. He told us how the Rat Pack—Dean Martin, Sammy Davis, Jr., Frank Sinatra, Peter Lawford, and Joey Bishop—saw his show in Vegas.

Johnny was talented and kind. His daughter, Sharon Brown, also appeared on *Good Times* in 1977 on the "Breaker, Breaker" episode as fun girl Nancy Colton. Over the years, Johnny and I stayed in touch, even participating in autograph signings with the cast, until his passing on March 2, 2022.

Good Times, Ain't We Lucky We Got 'Em:
Memoir of an American Sweetheart

Sweet Daddy Williams: The Menacing Numbers Runner

Sweet Daddy Williams was a menacing neighborhood numbers runner and pimp, known for his flashy clothes and jewelry. Theodore Wilson, affectionately known as Teddy, portrayed the character of Sweet Daddy.

Working with Teddy Wilson was a wonderful experience. He was a trained actor who brought authenticity to the role, making Sweet Daddy both intimidating and strangely endearing. I thoroughly enjoyed watching him in rehearsals, particularly as he trained and developed his character.

Although I didn't engage in deep conversations with Teddy, he was always polite and a true gentleman on set. One moment that stands out in my memory occurred on tape night when my mom was visiting me. As we walked backstage, she passed by Teddy, and I noticed him giving her a double take, as if he wanted to speak to her. I smiled, knowing Mom didn't see his reaction, especially since she looked spectacular that night! Later, I told her about Teddy's double take, and she grinned.

Teddy had a knack for making those around him feel comfortable, which made working with him enjoyable. His portrayal of Sweet Daddy remains one of the most iconic roles on *Good Times*.

Looting Lenny: The Character Within a Character

Another unforgettable character from *Good Times* was Lenny, also known as Looting Lenny, who had plenty. Dap Sugar Willie, an actor who left a lasting impression on me on and off the set, brought this character to life.

Dap Sugar Willie was not just a great character to me, he was also a fantastic person to watch. I got a real kick out of watching him in rehearsal because it seemed like he was a character within a character. Even as a person, Dap Sugar Willie exuded a larger-than-life persona. Each day, he would come into rehearsal dressed in a sharp suit, with his hair always pressed and curled. He carried an attaché case where he kept his script and paperwork.

What stood out most was his meticulous attention to detail. Before taking a seat, Dap Sugar Willie would take out a white handkerchief, dust off his chair, spread the handkerchief on the seat, and then sit down. I thought it was the strangest thing, but that's just who he was. Once seated, he would cross his legs, with everything about him perfectly in place—his hair, clothes, shoes. Every day, he wore a different suit, coordinating shirt, and shoes. Let's just say he was sharp every single day.

Dap Sugar Willie was undoubtedly the best well-dressed actor on our set. His dedication to his appearance and his character made him stand out, and it was clear that he took pride in everything he did. Watching him was like witnessing a masterclass in character development, and it's something I'll never forget.

Moses Gunn as Carl Dixon

Moses Gunn played Carl Dixon, Florida's second husband, on *Good Times*. His arrival marked a significant shift in the Evans family dynamic and introduced a storyline that remains one of the series' most surprising and controversial elements.

When Moses joined the show, he brought new energy as Carl. However, there was always a sense that his character never genuinely blended with the family. This wasn't a reflection on Moses's performance—he was a phenomenal actor—but rather a result of how the character was written. Carl Dixon was an atheist, a stark contrast to Florida, who was a very religious woman. This difference surprised me, as I'm sure it was to many viewers as well. I didn't care for the idea of Florida marrying an atheist; it didn't align with the profoundly religious character that Esther Rolle had so beautifully portrayed. However, as an actress on the show, I had no say in the creative decisions made by the producers.

I never learned how Esther felt about the show's direction with Carl and Florida's relationship. But later, after the show had ended, I heard rumors that this storyline may have been one of the reasons Miss Rolle chose to leave the show for a year. Esther was deeply connected to her character and had strong feelings about the choices they made for Florida.

One of the aspects that disturbed Esther was the idea of her character leaving her three children to go to Arizona with Carl. She couldn't reconcile the Florida Evans she knew and loved with the woman who would abandon her teenage son, Michael, to run off with a man. Being a strong, principled woman, this storyline did not sit well with her. She felt it was out of character for Florida, and as the actress who had brought Florida to life, she did not agree with this choice.

These creative differences ultimately led to tension behind

the scenes. Esther's departure from the show was a significant moment, not just for the viewers but for all of us who worked with her. Her commitment to authenticity in her character made Florida Evans such an iconic and beloved figure in television history. It's a testament to Esther's integrity as an actress that she stood by her principles, even when it meant stepping away from a role that had defined her career.

Chip Fields: From Auditioning for Thelma to Portraying an Iconic Character

Chip Fields holds a special place in the history of *Good Times*. Along with me, Chip was one of the actresses who auditioned for the character of Thelma. While the role ultimately went to me, Chip would later return to the show to play a character who left a lasting impression on audiences everywhere.

As Ms. Gordon, Penny's no-nonsense mother, Chip's character was abusive—the mother who burned Penny with an iron. This shocking moment was powerful and introduced the issue of child abuse to television audiences for the very first time.

Chip played that character so well that it sent chills down your spine. Her performance was haunting, bringing an intensity and realism that were rare on TV at that time. The storyline eventually led to Willona adopting Penny as her daughter, providing a powerful, heartwarming resolution.

That groundbreaking episode pushed boundaries and opened meaningful conversations about child abuse, something that hadn't been widely discussed on television before. It marked a turning point for the show and the audience, demonstrating the power of television to address complex social issues and make a real impact.

Looking back, I'm grateful Chip was able to bring such depth to that role. Her unforgettable performance is a testament to her talent and her courage in taking on such a challenging and vital character.

CHAPTER 5

The Minds Behind the Magic: The Creative Team

The Creators: Eric Monte and Michael Evans

Eric Monte and Michael Evans were the pioneering visionaries behind our beloved *Good Times*. Without their creativity, the show wouldn't have existed as we know it. Their collaboration stemmed from their life experiences and a shared commitment to authentically showcasing Black family life on television. Before the show's inception, they navigated challenging journeys to Hollywood, ultimately achieving success and fulfillment along the way.

Eric Monte, born Kenneth Williams in Chicago in 1943, grew up in the Cabrini-Green housing projects, where he witnessed firsthand the struggles and triumphs of urban Black families that inspired his writing. In the 1960s, he moved to Hollywood, determined to break into the entertainment industry and transform the portrayal of Black families on television.

Good Times, Ain't We Lucky We Got 'Em:
Memoir of an American Sweetheart

Eric Monte, co-creator of Good Times.

Michael Evans, co-creator of Good Times.

In 1971, Eric created *Cooley High*, a coming-of-age film inspired by his teenage experiences. The film's success enabled him to pitch the concept of *Good Times* to Norman Lear, to portray a strong Black family—a narrative rarely seen on TV then. Eric's vision of a working-class Black family tackling real-life issues was innovative and became the heart of our show.

Michael Evans was more than just an actor who portrayed Lionel Jefferson on *All in the Family*, a role that transitioned into *The Jeffersons*. Born in North Carolina and raised in California, he had a deep connection to his roots and the struggles faced by African Americans across the country. He moved to Hollywood as a young man interested in acting and writing. Through *All in the Family*, he connected with Norman Lear and began developing ideas with Eric. Their partnership was crucial. While Eric's storytelling grounded the show in authentic Black experiences, Michael contributed his acting and writing expertise, adding character development and ensuring relatable and impactful storylines. Michael's name is all over the show in our TV family's surname and the character of Michael Evans. Together, they presented the idea of our show that would portray a Black family from a more positive and honest perspective, and that's when the magic took shape.

Eric was always present on set, keeping a close eye on his creation. He had a consistent routine to ensure everything stayed true to the essence of the Evans family and the stories we told. I met Eric during the first week of rehearsals for the show; he would check in to see how our rehearsals were going each week. On Fridays, Eric listened to the script reading, ensuring it made sense according to his vision for our show. He listened and then gave his opinion. Eric's dedication to the show was clear in every script and moment on screen. His presence ensured that *Good Times* entertained and carried a deeper meaning, reflecting the reality of many families like ours. They also made significant contributions to television beyond *Good Times*. Eric wrote and produced on other shows like *The Jeffersons* and *What's Happening!*

Eric's and Michael's commitment to portraying the realities of poor, working-class Black communities made our show entertaining and socially relevant. Their storytelling captured the essence of our struggles and triumphs, touching viewers' hearts nationwide. Their work invited African American culture to the national table and corrected harmful narratives about what it meant to be Black in America. Eric and Michael grabbed the opportunity given to them by the Civil Rights Movement and used it to uplift communities of color nationwide. They were staunch allies.

Eric and Michael were integral to our show, and the backbone of many shows that shaped television during that era. Their legacy as creators continues to inspire storytellers and audiences alike. Their impact on television, particularly in showcasing African American experiences, remains a testament to their talent and vision.

Norman Lear: The Visionary Producer

Norman Lear was the executive producer and co-creator of *Good Times*. He played a pivotal role in shaping the show's direction and content, focusing on the struggles and triumphs of an African American family living in a public housing project in Chicago. Lear's commitment to addressing social issues through comedy was a hallmark of his productions, and *Good Times* was no exception. The show tackled topics like poverty, racism, and family dynamics, making it a significant part of the television landscape during the 1970s.

Groundbreaking television does not come without opposition. In the 2016 documentary, *Norman Lear: Just Another Version Of You,* Norman talked about a meeting with

Norman Lear, executive producer and co-creator of Good Times.

the Black Panthers: "One day, three members of the Black Panthers stormed into my offices at CBS, saying they'd 'Come to see the garbage man. *Good Times* was garbage,' they said, and on they ranted. 'Shows nothing but a white man's version of a Black family. The character of J.J. is a put-down. Every time you see a Black man on the tube, he is dirt poor, wears shit clothes, can't afford nothing. We got Black men in America doing better than most whites.' "I said, 'Hold on, hold on, hold on. Okay, let's talk.' And that may have had as much to do as anything else with the 'Why don't we make *The Jeffersons*'" (*Norman Lear: Just* Another *Version of You*, 00:52:40-00:53:38).

Norman's guidance and creative insight shaped our characters and storylines. His belief in authentic representation through storytelling empowered us as actors and deeply connected with audiences nationwide. He co-founded People For the American Way, a progressive advocacy organization, and has been a staunch advocate for social justice and civil liberties throughout his career. His contributions to entertainment and activism have earned him numerous awards and honors, including multiple Emmy Awards and the prestigious Peabody Award.

A Consummate Professional

Norman was a cool guy. You never saw him sweat. He never got out of character, even when he didn't like something—he remained quiet and made changes. The second director of our show (I won't mention names) did not know what he was doing. He had the cast line up behind the couch most of the time. The movements he had us making were unnatural. So, on a Tuesday afternoon, Norman came down to see the run-through, and we lined up behind the couch, moving oddly. The cast felt embarrassed because we knew what the directors should do. At the end of the run-through, Norman asked the director to gather his things and step outside with him. A few minutes later, Norman returned to the rehearsal hall alone. We never saw that director again. Norman was smooth and never missed a beat. He handled the matter. Norman dismissed the cast and announced we'd have a new director the next day.

My working relationship with Norman was excellent. Kind and respectful to everyone on set, he and I were huggers, so we often greeted one another with a warm embrace. He was an active listener, which made the people feel unique and important. Further, *Good Times* came off the heels of some excellent white shows. Norman treated our show and cast with the same professionalism, respect, and integrity that he had given those shows, like *Maude*. I was grateful to have this kind of experience and atmosphere.

I couldn't have asked for a better boss for my first acting job. Norman was a class act and a safe person for us. Being young and vulnerable, I moved across the country, away from everything and everyone I had ever known. Someone in

power with bad intentions could have taken advantage of me. I consider myself extremely blessed and fortunate that it was not the case. I hit the jackpot by working with Norman. He created a safe environment for the young people under his care.

Other times, we saw the lighter side of Norman, especially at our cast parties. Norman had this comedic way that he sang for us. He *always* sang "My Funny Valentine." It was *how* he sang it that made us laugh. When he sang, he used a head movement to create a vibrating effect instead of producing a natural vibrato with his voice. One would have to see it to appreciate its comedy. Trust me, it was funny and made us crack up. Norman was cerebral, so he usually looked deep in thought. He was a quiet man with a great sense of humor. I had the honor of attending his one-hundredth birthday party. He hugged me and thanked me for being a wonderful person.

Norman Lear's impact on television and society continues to resonate. His dedication to using the power of storytelling to foster understanding and empathy remains a guiding light in the entertainment industry. His legacy as a trailblazer and visionary ensures that his influence will endure for generations. Thanks for the memories, Norman.

Good Times, Ain't We Lucky We Got 'Em:
Memoir of an American Sweetheart

Guiding the Moments: The Directors Who Shaped Good Times

Herbert Kenwith

Born on July 14, 1917, in New Jersey, Herbert Kenwith's journey into entertainment began with a passion for storytelling and a sharp eye for visual aesthetics. His directorial style was a deft balance of technical precision and emotional depth, seamlessly weaving together intricate narratives with compelling performances.

Herb was the original director of *Good Times* and also contributed his talents to *The Jeffersons*, *All in the Family*, *Diff'rent Strokes*, *Sanford and Son*, and the list goes on. He brought a special touch to the set, making working with him an absolute pleasure. There was something about Herb—he was cool, diplomatic, and had a deft way of handling actors with finesse. A true professional, Herb effortlessly balanced the demands of directing with the relational dynamics at play.

Herb possessed an extraordinary ability to be both direct and lenient, creating a directing experience pleasant for everyone involved. I've always believed that effective directing transcends technical skills; it's about understanding people and their personalities. Herb embodied this philosophy perfectly. He knew how to navigate the complexities of working with different actors, ensuring each felt valued and understood.

Perhaps Herb's mastery of the art of directing stemmed from his roots in the old school of filmmaking. He had a fascinating connection to the legendary actress Mae West, known for her iconic line, "Why don't you come up and see me sometime?" Just knowing this connection added depth to Herb's legacy.

On tape nights, when the pressure was on and we made mistakes, Herb remained the epitome of professionalism. If any of us made a mistake during a scene in front of a live audience, Herb smoothly intervened, seamlessly blending the error into the retake process. His calm demeanor and quick thinking ensured that the show went on flawlessly, leaving the audience none the wiser.

Herb was a director who fiercely protected his actors, shielding us from any unnecessary scrutiny or embarrassment. His unwavering support and dedication to our craft made him an invaluable asset to the show. With Herb at the helm, we felt confident and secure, knowing that he had our backs no matter what.

In the directing world, Herb was genuinely one-of-a-kind. His legacy lives on in the timeless episodes of *Good Times* and in the hearts of all who worked with him. Herb set the bar high for directors everywhere, proving that true greatness lies in skill, compassion, and empathy.

The name "Mae West" was familiar, though I was young then. It wasn't until I met her that I truly understood the depth of her impact. Our introduction took place at a lavish dinner event that Herb had expertly arranged. As Mae West descended the escalator, she radiated timeless elegance, her petite frame enveloped in pristine white attire. Remarkably, despite being at least eighty, she showed no signs of age—no wrinkles or blemishes—just smooth, ageless beauty.

At the time, I couldn't fully grasp why someone as esteemed as Mae West would want to meet me. However, as I've matured, I've come to realize that she recognized qualities in me that I hadn't yet seen in myself. Perhaps it was my authenticity or my warm spirit that drew her in. Whatever the reason, Mae West looked beyond the character of Thelma and saw the person behind it—a kind-hearted individual with a generous spirit.

Our encounter was memorable, albeit surprising in its quiet intimacy. On-screen and in her films, Mae West exuded confidence and charisma, yet in person, she was surprisingly reserved. Nevertheless, her talent and impact on the entertainment industry were undeniable, spanning decades from her teenage years.

Meeting Mae West was one of many encounters I had during those days with stars from Hollywood's golden era. Jack Benny, Loretta Young, and Lucille Ball were among the luminaries I had the pleasure of meeting at various events. Each encounter left a lasting impression, whether Loretta Young's beauty and grace or Lucille Ball's playful humor.

Lucille Ball's response to meeting me and my brother was particularly memorable. With a twinkle in her eye, she quipped, "I babysat you, dear." It was a line she may have used with many, but at that moment, it made us feel special as if we shared a connection that transcended time and fame.

In hindsight, those encounters with Hollywood legends were glamorous events and opportunities to connect with icons who had left an indelible mark on the entertainment industry. Meeting Mae West and others from Hollywood's golden era was a privilege and a reminder of the enduring legacy of those who came before us.

Good Times, Ain't We Lucky We Got 'Em:
Memoir of an American Sweetheart

Gerren Keith

Gerren Keith, a prominent TV director, and the first African American director on *Good Times*, made a significant impact on our show as the third and final director of the series. With a deep passion for storytelling and a keen eye for detail, Gerren's remarkable journey solidified his place in television history. Although he joined the show later in its run, his arrival brought a fresh perspective and energy that revitalized our work. We were fortunate to have this outstanding director join our cast during such a pivotal time.

Gerren's career in television spanned several decades, a testament to his dedication and hard work. Starting as a production assistant, Gerren quickly rose through the ranks, showcasing his talent and expertise behind the camera. In the realm of television, Gerren's name became synonymous with excellence. His directorial style was characterized by precision and creativity. Under his direction, our performances were elevated, and we infused scenes with energy, emotion, and depth. Whether tackling social issues or exploring family dynamics, Gerren approached every script with integrity and vision.

One of Gerren's greatest strengths as a director was his exceptional ability to connect with actors on a personal level. He cultivated a collaborative environment on set, encouraging creativity and empowering us to deliver our best performances. Behind the camera, Gerren's passion for storytelling shone through in every frame, earning him respect and admiration in our industry.

Working with Gerren was a joy. He strictly adhered to the rules of directing, and everything ran smoothly and efficiently during filming. As time passed, we all grew to appreciate and respect his dedication to his craft. Under his direction, the show's last two years were a pleasant and productive time for all of us. He brought a sense of professionalism and camaraderie to the set, ensuring we continued delivering quality performances until the very end.

Gerren Keith continues to inspire generations of filmmakers and television enthusiasts alike. His work on *Good Times* was a fitting conclusion to a show that meant so much to many. His influence on the industry endures.

Good Times, Ain't We Lucky We Got 'Em:
Memoir of an American Sweetheart

Allan Manings: A Legacy in Television Comedy

Most people understand the role of the director in a play, TV show, or film. However, many people may not widely understand a producer's role. For those who don't know, the producer hires staff for the production: the director, crew, and sometimes the cast, and coordinates the activities of the writers, directors, managers, and actors. Raising money and setting the budget and size of the production are other responsibilities.

Allan Manings was a distinguished figure in television comedy, having also worked as a director and writer. A passionate storyteller, Allan began his career writing for television in the 1960s. His sharp wit and keen understanding of humor quickly garnered attention, leading to collaborations with influential producers and directors. In the early 1970s, Manings joined forces with Norman Lear, a partnership that proved to be transformative. They were the co-creators of *Good Times*.

As a director, Allan brought a unique blend of creativity and precision to our show. His keen eye for comedic timing and his ability to nurture our casts' talents contributed significantly to its success. Norman and Allan shaped our show's distinctive voice, balancing humor with social commentary in a way that resonated with audiences across America.

I felt Allan was the person who wanted me to be on *Good Times* the most, especially during my Hollywood audition. During that first audition, Allan approached me before I walked onto the set to do my lines. He said, "I would like you to hit this word this way..." (There was a word he wanted me to say a certain way.)

When I got to that word, I said it exactly the way he told me to. I believe he was testing me to see if I could follow directions *and* if I would hit a comedic line in a certain way. I *hit* that word precisely the way he asked me, and I believe that helped to win me the part of Thelma Evans.

After *Good Times*, Allan continued to make significant contributions to television. His career spanned several decades, during which he wrote and directed for many shows, showcasing his versatility and commitment to quality entertainment. Allan's impact on television comedy remains profound. His dedication to authenticity and talent for crafting memorable characters and storylines solidified his reputation as a visionary in the industry, leaving a profound impact on television comedy.

Writers

Kim Weiskopf and Roger Shulman formed a dynamic writing team that influenced the dialogue and humor on *Good Times*. Their collaboration brought wit and authenticity to the show, helping to craft some of the most memorable lines that still resonate with audiences today. Kim's and Roger's ability to capture the essence of the characters and their experiences helped give the Evans family a relatable voice, making each episode genuine and heartfelt.

Their skillful writing reflected the cultural and social challenges of the time, yet always maintained warmth and humor that kept audiences engaged. They helped to ensure that *Good Times* balanced comedy and the serious topics it often addressed.

I cannot overstate Kim Weiskopf's and Roger Shulman's contributions to the show's success, as their collaboration behind the scenes played a pivotal role in the longevity and cultural relevance of *Good Times*.

CHAPTER 6

Cameos and Connections: The Stars Who Graced Our Set

Over the five years that *Good Times* was on the air, we had the privilege of sharing our stage with remarkable actors. It would take another book to reminisce about *all* of them, so I will share a few here and send a warm "thank you" to every bright star who graced our set.

Comedy Behind the Scenes: Jay Leno's Stand-Up Visit

Recalling Jay Leno's time on the show brings back memories of laughter and camaraderie. Before becoming the iconic late-night host we know today, Jay made a guest appearance on *Good Times* that left a lasting impression on us. He was an extra who briefly conversed with J.J. in a free clinic. It was one of his earliest television appearances. Jay brought his trademark wit and humor to the set. His energy was infectious, and he had a way of lightening the mood during filming breaks.

Good Times, Ain't We Lucky We Got 'Em:
Memoir of an American Sweetheart

Jay Leno made a guest appearance as an extra on Good Times, where he appeared in a scene with J.J. at a free clinic.

Off-camera, Jay chatted with everyone, offering encouragement and advice to those of us starting in the industry. He shared jokes and stories with the cast and crew, creating a sense of warmth and fun on set. His passion for comedy was evident, and he was always eager to discuss the craft and share insights from his experiences. As stated earlier in the Jimmie Walker chapter, Jay was one of Jimmie's stand-up comedy writers, so he knew comedy.

Eventually, Jay's career soared to new heights, becoming the host of *The Tonight Show with Jay Leno*, a position he held for over two decades, solidifying his place in television history. His comedic timing and engaging interviews made him a beloved figure on late-night television. His success extended beyond television. He continued to perform stand-up comedy, touring nationally and internationally. His observational humor and ability to connect with audiences resonated across generations, earning him accolades and recognition as one of the most influential comedians of his time. Known for his passion for automobiles, Jay has a notable collection of cars and is actively involved in the automotive community, hosting shows and events that celebrate classic cars and automotive culture.

I'm grateful for the opportunity to have worked alongside such a talented and genuine individual. His contributions to comedy and television continue to inspire, and his influence as a comedian and entertainer remains vibrant.

Comedy Quartet

Popo, played by Randy Martin, alongside TK Carter as Head, Larry Beecham as Cool Breeze, and of course, Jimmie Walker as J.J., formed a memorable quartet on *Good Times* as the Awesome Foursome. Their debut on November 2, 1977 introduced a fun and engaging element to the show. They were a hilarious and charming ensemble who created lighthearted yet meaningful scenes.

Popo constantly pursued Thelma, making for some humorous and relatable moments. His character was persistent

Good Times, Ain't We Lucky We Got 'Em:
Memoir of an American Sweetheart

The Awesome Foursome
(L to R): TK Carter, Jimmie Walker, Larry Beecham, Randy Martin

and playful, always trying to win her affection, but with a sense of innocence that kept things light. The camaraderie between Popo and the rest of the foursome—Head, Cool Breeze, and J.J.—was magnetic. TK's portrayal of Head was marked by his comedic timing, while Larry's Cool Breeze added a level of laid-back charisma that complemented J.J.'s larger-than-life persona. Off-screen, all the guys were incredibly professional, down-to-earth, and enjoyable to be around. Their presence on set always brought a sense of fun, and I remember looking forward to the days when they would film. They were a group that not only delivered laughs but also reflected a sense of brotherhood that resonated with the audience.

A Childhood Star All Grown Up—Stymie Beard's Return to the Screen

Stymie Beard, playing the role of Monty, a friend of James.

Matthew "Stymie" Beard brought his unique charm and humor to the character of Monty, a friend of James and a regular presence in our neighborhood. Stymie Beard, known for his distinctive style and comedic timing, brought lighthearted moments to *Good Times*. On set, Stymie was a joy to work with. His energy was infectious, and he made everyone smile with his quick wit and playful banter.

Stymie was a kind man, and we were all super excited to have him on the set with us because he was one of the little rascals. I remember how I felt seeing him for the first time. He was a lot like on *The Little Rascals*: calm, genuine, and warm-hearted with that infectious smile. He naturally connected with people and often shared stories and jokes that entertained us between takes. He quickly bonded with our cast, creating a supportive environment where we actors thrived.

Beyond *Good Times*, Stymie had a varied career in entertainment. His talent and versatility allowed him to transition seamlessly between different roles and genres throughout his career. Stymie was involved in community outreach and charitable endeavors, using his platform to support causes close to his heart. The world continues to remember and celebrate him for his dedication to his craft and impact on audiences.

Roscoe Lee Browne: A Poignant Presence as Reverend Sam

Roscoe Lee Browne's portrayal of Reverend Sam, James Evans's old Army buddy, added a poignant and respectful dimension to *Good Times*. His character brought wisdom, integrity, and spirituality to the storyline, profoundly influencing the lives of the Evans family. Reverend Sam wasn't just a guest character but a beacon of guidance, offering solace and perspective during challenging times. He resonated deeply with the characters and audience.

Working alongside Roscoe was transformational. He embodied the role with a blend of gravitas and compassion,

Roscoe Lee Browne plays Reverend Sam, an old Army friend of James.

making his character authentic. The way he delivered his lines with such weight and sincerity made every interaction I experienced with his character profound.

Behind the scenes, Roscoe was a consummate professional and generous mentor, who brought a wealth of experience from his extensive film, television, and theater career. His presence was uplifting, creating a supportive environment where creativity flourished and performances elevated. Roscoe's dedication to his craft and willingness to help others grow as actors made him a cherished figure among the cast and crew.

Roscoe's accomplishments spanned a wide range of roles and achievements. Films such as *The Cowboys, Logan's Run*, and *Moon 44* showcased his versatility and talent as an actor. His distinctive voice also made him a sought-after narrator and voice actor, lending his talents to documentaries, animated series, and audiobooks. Outside of acting, Roscoe was a poet, playwright, and educator who used his platform to advocate for social justice and equality. His eloquence and intellect made him a respected figure on and off the screen, leaving a legacy in the entertainment industry and beyond.

I am grateful I got to work with Roscoe. He influenced my acting, and his impact on *Good Times* was more than just a role; he offered guidance and an anchor on a show that aimed to reflect the struggles and triumphs of everyday life.

A Memorable Collaboration with Philip Michael Thomas

Working with Philip Michael Thomas on *Good Times* was an experience that remains dear to my heart. Philip, who portrayed Wise, Thelma's first boyfriend, left a lasting impression on and off the screen. Despite the characters' age differences—Thelma at sixteen and Wise at twenty-one—their dynamic was compelling, adding depth to the show's exploration of young love and the challenges of growing up. Wise's quirky endeavor of writing essays on sexual behavior in the ghetto introduced a unique layer to the show's narrative.

With Philip Michael Thomas on a fashion photo shoot for Right On! magazine.

It was amusing to watch the characters speculate about authorship, unaware that it was Philip's character behind the words.

Philip was not only an exceptional actor but also an extremely handsome gentleman. His charm and charisma made every scene fun, and he brought professionalism and dedication that was truly admirable. Working alongside him was a pleasure, and I appreciated the opportunity to share the screen with someone who was so naturally talented. Despite *Good Times* being his first TV appearance, Philip's acting skills were undeniable. From the start, he possessed immense talent. My intuition told me he was destined for greatness, and indeed, he achieved remarkable success with roles in *Dreamgirls* and *Miami Vice*. My belief in his potential was vindicated, and I am proud to have acted with such a talented individual during his formative years in the industry.

Our collaboration extended beyond the set of *Good Times* when *Right On!* magazine asked us to do a fashion shoot. I fondly remember that day, wearing beautiful outfits and posing next to Philip. He was a true gentleman, and the experience of working together in a different context only strengthened my admiration for him.

Philip's real-life role as a husband and devoted father to three beautiful daughters added depth to his character. Witnessing his love and dedication to his family was admirable, and caused me to respect him even more. This was also why Philip and I had never dated. Over the years, there has been speculation about whether we were a couple off-screen. No, we were not. However, if he had been available, I would have been interested. I mean, have you seen him?

Philip Michael Thomas was more than just Thelma's first boyfriend on the show; he was a wonderful person and a talented actor who brought something special to *Good Times*. I am elated that I got to work with him and witness firsthand the beginning of a remarkable career.

Johnny Sekka's Royal Presence

Johnny Sekka, who played Ibe (pronounced Ebay) Wubila, an African prince, embarked on a remarkable journey that took him from the vibrant streets of West Africa to the glitz and glamour of Hollywood. Born in Dakar, Senegal, Johnny's life and career were a testament to his versatility and talent. Before his guest appearance on *Good Times*, Johnny had already built a distinguished career on both sides of the Atlantic, appearing in stage productions, films, and television shows. His ability to transition seamlessly between genres and characters made him a celebrated figure in the entertainment industry.

Challenging Stereotypes and Celebrating Africa

Through his portrayal of Ibe Wubila, Johnny entertained audiences, challenged stereotypes, and celebrated the richness of African culture. This storyline marked the first time African culture was prominently featured on national television, which was incredibly exciting for the cast. We were eager to bring this informative and culturally diverse show to our audiences. It was delightful because it centered on Thelma falling in love with an African prince.

Working with Johnny was an unparalleled experience. His presence on set was not just transformative, it was downright inspiring. From the moment he stepped onto the soundstage, he brought the professionalism, passion, and authenticity that raised the bar for us all. I witnessed Johnny's dedication to his craft and unwavering commitment to excellence. His humility matched his talent, and his generosity knew no bounds. Whether offering encouragement between takes or sharing invaluable insights into the nuances of performance, Johnny was always there, lifting me and the entire cast to new heights. Having Johnny on set was a captivating experience. His commanding presence and strong acting skills were remarkable to witness. During rehearsals, his beautiful African accent added an extra layer of authenticity to his character, though it occasionally made understanding him a bit challenging. One charming quirk was how he pronounced my character's name, Thelma, as "Delma."

African Culture Brought to Life

The production of this episode spanned two weeks, with the story unfolding in two parts. This format allowed for greater attention to detail and enabled me to experiment with my hairstyle. I worked closely with the hairdresser to design intricate braids that ideally suited my vision. It was gratifying to know that my hairstyles on the show inspired young girls to emulate them.

We also had the chance to wear authentic African outfits, which added to the overall cultural immersion experience. From the vibrant colors to the intricate designs, wearing the garments was a beautiful experience for our cast. We indulged in authentic African cuisine, too, such as fufu (a starchy African side dish), and embraced cultural practices like sitting on low stools, just as it's done in Africa. The attention to detail in portraying African culture made this episode a memorable and enriching experience for the entire cast.

Beyond his remarkable talent and mentorship, Johnny was simply a joy to be around. His infectious laughter and genuine kindness made every day feel like a family reunion. Working alongside him felt less like a job and more like a masterclass in storytelling.

I am grateful for the opportunity to share the screen with such a remarkable talent and human being. Johnny Sekka's legacy lives on in the hearts of those who knew him and in the timeless performances he left behind for generations to enjoy. People will forever remember his portrayal of the African prince on *Good Times* as a culturally enriching moment in television history.

Sassy and Sharp: Helen Martin

Helen Martin as Weeping Wanda on Good Times.

Helen Martin, a seasoned actress known for her sharp wit and memorable presence, played Weeping Wanda, a cornerstone of our television family. Her signature sass and comedic timing, qualities that had already made her beloved in the entertainment world, marked Helen's role. Her rich, authentic portrayal made her indispensable to the fabric of our storyline. Working alongside Helen was a privilege. She embodied Wanda with a blend of wisdom, humor, and warmth that made her scenes unforgettable. Helen had this incredible ability to infuse her character with a depth of emotion that resonated deeply with audiences and castmates.

Wanda was a no-nonsense woman who didn't shy away from speaking her mind, and Helen's portrayal was hilarious and heartfelt. She connected to viewers by the way she interacted with the Evans family—quick quips and a sharp tongue, yet underneath it all, displaying her warmth.

Helen's ability to balance humor with depth made her character a memorable part of the *Good Times* legacy. Her presence on set was equally impactful—she was a professional who knew how to command a scene while still being a generous and supportive colleague. Helen reminded everyone of the importance of strong, dynamic female television characters.

Helen was a nurturing presence on set. Her maternal instinct extended beyond her role as Wanda, offering the other younger actors and me advice and support. Her wisdom and experience were invaluable, and she often shared stories from her extensive career in theater and television, inspiring us with her passion for the craft.

Helen had a remarkable career that spanned decades. She was a celebrated actress and a trailblazer in the industry. She was a dedicated activist and advocate for social justice, using her platform to raise awareness about important issues affecting African American communities. Her commitment to equality and representation paved the way for future generations of actors and artists.

Raymond Allen as Ned the Wino

Raymond Allan as Ned the Wino on Good Times.

Ned the Wino's role on the show was integral to exploring important themes by combining humor and depth. Raymond Allen's portrayal of Ned depicted a character who faced challenges with resilience and occasional moments of insight, offering a poignant reflection of life in our community.

Ned the Wino's interactions with the Evans family, particularly with characters like Willona and the kids, showcased his warmth and vulnerability. Despite his struggles with alcoholism, Ned's presence brought themes of humanity and compassion to the show. His friendship with the neighborhood and his occasional pearls of wisdom added a layer of authenticity to the storytelling, resonating deeply with viewers who appreciated his genuine portrayal.

Raymond was a talented actor. It amazed me how he could drop into the character of Ned the Wino at a moment's notice. Raymond did not drink, which surprises some people because of how well he portrayed Ned. He was a skilled performer and would talk to us as Raymond and then switch on the character of Ned. He could flip that switch in a heartbeat. This is an example of acting being a skill one must learn, cultivate, and practice.

You may remember that in the episode where J.J. painted "Black Jesus," Michael looked at the painting and said, "This is not Black Jesus. This is Ned the Wino."

That line stuck with audiences, as it was the first time anyone had ever called Jesus Black on television. Ned the Wino's face was representative of Black Jesus, pointing to a message of love for all skin colors and life conditions. This is just another way that our show pointed to the humanity of all.

Raymond approached his role with dedication and empathy, ensuring that he portrayed Ned's journey with authenticity and respect. His nuanced performance captured the complexities of Ned's character, highlighting the societal issues he represented while maintaining his dignity and humanity.

CHAPTER 7

The Brush, Rhythm, and Wardrobe: Coloring the Soul of Good Times

Ernie Barnes: *The Artist Who Painted Our World*

The artist behind J.J.'s iconic paintings, Ernie Barnes, brought a signature visual style that enriched our television family's home. His artwork, featured as J.J.'s paintings, captured the spirit and vibrancy of African American life with vivid colors and dynamic compositions. Each painting told a unique story, reflecting our characters' joys, struggles, and resilience.

With their authentic representation and cultural pride, Ernie's paintings resonated deeply with our show's audience. His artwork, a visual narrative that complemented the storytelling, was more than just paintings. It was a mirror that reflected the viewers' experiences and cultural identities.

Ernie would come to the set at least once a week or every two weeks when he had to do a painting for the show. He

Good Times, Ain't We Lucky We Got 'Em:
Memoir of an American Sweetheart

Word-renowned artist, Ernie Barnes.

was always one who you never saw sweat. He was a friendly, cool guy, large yet quiet. He occasionally invited the cast to his home for dinner. I once had dinner with him and his wife, whose name also happened to be Bernadette.

Ernie was a renowned artist whose career extended long after *Good Times*. He gained recognition for his unique style, known as "Neo-Mannerism," characterized by elongated figures and exaggerated poses that conveyed movement and emotion. His paintings often depicted scenes of everyday life in African American communities, celebrating the beauty and strength of his subjects.

Ernie's artistry became widely celebrated in the art world, exhibiting his paintings in galleries and museums nationwide, garnering acclaim for their cultural significance and artistic merit. His influence as an artist grew, inspiring generations of artists and admirers alike.

Ernie's accomplishments as an artist spanned beyond the canvas. His influence on popular culture, his dedication to portraying African American life through art, and his notable commissions, including the official painting for the 1984 Summer Olympics in Los Angeles, all contributed to cementing his legacy as a leader in the art world.

Ernie's impact on *Good Times* remains a testament to his artistic vision and ability to capture our community in his paintings. His contributions to television and the arts continue. Eddie Murphy purchased Ernie's original painting, *The Sugar Shack*, which graced the opening of our show, and the cover of Marvin Gaye's 1976 album, *I Want You*, from Marvin Gaye's estate for a mere $50,000 in 1984. However, Ernie painted a duplicate of *The Sugar Shack*, which sold at Christie's auction house in May 2022 for $15.2 million. That is seventy-six times the estimated price (auctioneers expected it to sell for $150,000 to $200,000). The buyer wanted to own a piece of his childhood. *Good Times* represents that kind of nostalgia for so many.

Adella Farmar: Fashionista

Now, let's chat wardrobe. Adella Farmar, our wardrobe designer, shaped our show's iconic fashion. She was a talented costume designer and a pioneer in an industry often segregated during the 1970s. Adella learned to sew at a young age from her mother, which sparked her lifelong passion for fashion. After studying at Manual Arts High School and Los Angeles Trade Technical College, she designed clothing for well-known celebrities like Lena Horne, Eartha Kitt, and Diahann Carroll.

The cast had insisted on hiring Black staff behind the scenes, which led to Adella's involvement. I worked closely with her to create Thelma's signature look. The perfectly tailored costumes Adella made accentuated Thelma's style.

Adella had an incredible eye for selecting colors that embodied each character's personality and style. John Amos often donned neutral tones—beige pants and brown shirts—which reflected his grounded, fatherly presence. Conversely, Esther radiated in vibrant hues like oranges, reds, and yellows, echoing Florida's strength and warmth. Jimmie Walker embraced his signature style with blue jeans and that unforgettable burgundy turtleneck, a staple of J.J.'s eccentric persona. Ja'Net favored brighter colors, especially yellows and greens, while Ralph's wardrobe consisted mostly of earthy tones like brown, green, and yellow.

Good Times, Ain't We Lucky We Got 'Em:
Memoir of an American Sweetheart

Adella Farmar with Esther Rolle

These thoughtful choices were far from random. Adella curated them to complement each actor's complexion and enhance the visual impact of our characters on screen, adding depth and personality to their portrayal.

For Thelma, Adella dressed me in elegant yet youthful shades of blue, purple, and burgundy. However, finding a comfortable style for me was a challenge that Adella handled like an innovative professional.

As a dancer from New York, I kept my New York style even though I lived in Los Angeles. When we were out, we always wore leotards with our dance pants. That was our usual outfit when running around the city to our dance classes.

Those clothes were skin-tight but easy to get into with no fuss. I only wore tight clothes because they felt the most comfortable on me. I also loved to wear high heels. Girls in their early teens in the mid-seventies wore high heels, usually platform shoes. In dance class, we wore flat shoes, but I always wore heels.

There I was in Hollywood, where Thelma had to wear mostly jeans like most teens. Adella bought our outfits for the show in Century City. They had beautiful quality clothes, but none of them fit me comfortably. Adella and I came up with a solution. She bought me some very nice burgundy platform shoes that gave me a high heel feeling. Then she bought me a few pairs of jeans and some blouses that a girl who lived in the projects of Chicago would wear.

"Let's see what we can do with these things to make you feel comfortable," she said.

Adella and I worked together on what I liked, which for me meant altering the jeans by sewing down the outside and inside seams all the way to the knees. I asked her to remove all the pockets and sew them flat, creating a smooth surface on all sides. She also added darts to the front, back, and sides of my tops, giving them a perfectly fitted, glove-like appearance. My work clothes became a second skin, much like my dance attire, and I finally felt comfortable. I also wore pantyhose under the pants to create a smooth silhouette.

Well, what do you know? I started a trend with my new and improved wardrobe with girls all over the country who looked up to me and wanted to dress like me. The tight jeans, sweaters, and blouses became fashion back then, and women still dress that way today.

Thelma introduced tight jeans to our American audience. Before Thelma, there were no such fitted clothes. I created the tight jeans and fitted tops out of the need for my clothes to fit, like dance wear, and Adella's knowledge and acceptance of what looked best for me on the show. No one has ever given the show credit for being the true innovator of that look, which is everywhere today, so I must give credit where credit is due.

Adella and I were close until she passed away in September 2022 at ninety-one. Adella's contributions extended beyond fashion, as she broke racial barriers in Hollywood. Her work helped define the fashion of the 1970s and 1980s, making her an essential part of television history.

Jim Gilstrap: Singer

Jim Gilstrap is a songwriter and one of the singers of the theme song for *Good Times*. His impact as the show's songwriter moved our television family. He enriched our storytelling with soulful and uplifting songs, bringing profound emotional depth to our characters' experiences. His ability to craft music that captured the show's spirit made him indispensable to our production.

BernNadette with Jim Gilstrap in 2023.

Jim was also a dedicated artist whose talent extended beyond *Good Times*. He was renowned for his powerful and soulful vocals, which graced recordings and collaborations with iconic musicians like Stevie Wonder, Elton John, Quincy Jones, and Barry White.

Jim's musical talents added richness and emotion to our storytelling, making our experiences on *Good Times* more vibrant and memorable. His legacy as a versatile and influential musician remains a cherished part of our television journey.

In 2007, I had the chance to meet Jim Gilstrap at a book signing event in Chicago where he was performing with the band Loose Ends. Jim identified himself as the co-singer of the *Good Times* theme song, clarifying that he performed it with Sondra "Blinky" Williams. Even though we only talked briefly, he informed me about some confusion with the lyrics.

I mentioned to him that I was aware of the confusion, but I never fully grasped the correct line. Jim clarified that the belief of the line being "hanging in a chow line" since the 1970s was a long-standing mistake. I concurred, stating that the phrase "hanging in a chow line" had always sounded peculiar to me. I initially thought it could be a reference to waiting in a welfare line because "chow line" didn't seem logical.

According to Jim, the confusion possibly originated from *The Dave Chappelle Show*, when Dave Chappelle said, "Hanging in a chow line." Chappelle might have gotten the lyrics online. Jim explained that the actual lyric is "hanging in and jivin'," sung by Sondra "Blinky" Williams.

Surprisingly, Jim mentioned that they removed other lines written for the *Good Times* theme song. I had no idea there were extra lyrics. Upon asking him what they were, he responded:

"Roaches roaming the hallways,

The landlord is nobody's fool,

He lives on the other side of town.

Good times."

Jim clarified that they chose not to include these lyrics to prevent any offense to Black audiences.

In 2015, I asked Jim and Gloria, his wife, to join me at the Hollywood Show in Burbank, California, to meet the cast of *Good Times*. The experience was enjoyable, particularly listening to Ja'Net DuBois and Jim Gilstrap discuss their historic theme songs. Ja'Net composed and performed the theme song for *The Jeffersons*, titled "Movin' On Up." She mentioned that they removed some of the lyrics in her song, but the specific ones are unknown to me.

In 2023, I realized I hadn't heard from Jim in a while, so I decided to stop by his house to check on him. That's when I learned about Jim's stroke in 2019. Thanks to Gloria's exceptional care, he is doing much better today. Jim is prominently featured on my Instagram, and we still maintain a strong bond.

Sondra "Blinky" Williams: Singer

Blinky Williams, another songwriter who sang the theme song along with Jim, contributed creatively to our series, and had a notable career beyond television. Blinky's accomplishments extend into the realm of music production and composition. Known for her ability to craft songs that resonated with diverse audiences, she blended elements of soul, funk, and R&B into her compositions.

Besides her work on television, Blinky collaborated with various artists and musicians, showcasing her diverse talent in the music industry. Her ability to write and produce music that crossed genres and connected with listeners highlighted her expert songwriting and composing skills.

Good Times, Ain't We Lucky We Got 'Em:
Memoir of an American Sweetheart

Sondra "Blinky" Williams

Dave Grusin: Composer

Dave Grusin's role as the composer for our show added a distinct musical flavor that enhanced the dynamics of our television family. His compositions were integral to setting the mood and atmosphere of our scenes, from moments of humor to heartfelt family interactions.

Dave was renowned for his work as a composer on our show and his prolific film-scoring career. He composed music for many iconic movies, such as *The Graduate, On Golden*

Pond, *Tootsie*, and *The Fabulous Baker Boys*. His ability to create memorable and emotionally resonant scores earned him awards and nominations, including an Academy Award for Best Original Score for *The Milagro Beanfield War* and a Grammy for his work on the soundtrack of *The Firm*.

Dave was also a highly respected jazz pianist and composer. He founded GRP Records, a jazz record label that became a significant force in the jazz industry, releasing albums by legendary artists such as Chick Corea, Lee Ritenour, and Diane Schuur. His contributions to jazz music earned him multiple Grammys, solidifying his status as an influential figure in the genre. His compositions transcended boundaries, resonated with audiences worldwide, and impacted the music industry.

Alan and Marilyn Bergman: Lyricists

Alan and Marilyn Bergman's contributions as lyricists for our show were more than just adding words to music. They had a unique ability to interpret our characters' experiences and emotions through their songwriting, giving a poetic dimension to our stories, and making our on-screen moments meaningful and relatable. The Bergman's ability to craft lyrics with family, love, and resilience themes elevated our storytelling. Their contributions added emotional depth to our characters' journeys, making their songs integral to the narrative.

Good Times, Ain't We Lucky We Got 'Em:
Memoir of an American Sweetheart

Beyond *Good Times*, Alan and Marilyn achieved remarkable success in the music industry. They are renowned for prolific collaborations with composers such as Michel Legrand, Marvin Hamlisch, and Dave Grusin. Together, they wrote lyrics for iconic songs performed by legendary artists like Barbra Streisand, Frank Sinatra, and Tony Bennett.

The Bergman's achievements include winning multiple Academy Awards for Best Original Song, including "The Windmills of Your Mind" from *The Thomas Crown Affair* and "The Way We Were" from the movie of the same name. Their songwriting talent solidified their status as preeminent film and famous music lyricists.

BernNadette Stanis with Brittany Rose

Good Times
Theme Song Lyrics

Any time you meet a payment.
Good times.

Any time you need a friend.
Good times.

Any time you're out from under.
Not getting hassled, not getting hustled.

Keepin' your head above water,
Making a wave when you can.

Temporary layoffs.
Good times.

Easy credit rip-offs.
Good times.

Scratchin' and surviving.
Good times.

Hanging in and jivin'.
Good times.

Ain't we lucky we got 'em.
Good times.

CHAPTER 8

*Behind the Scenes with Thelma:
Your Questions Answered*

Wherever I go, fans consistently ask about their favorite character or episode and behind-the-scenes gossip. While there is true and false information on the Internet, fans want to get the scoop straight from Thelma. Throughout this book, I answer many of the questions that fans have asked me over the years. Many of you asked questions in response to my request for them on my Instagram account—*thank you!*

Character Insights and Personal Experiences

QUESTION: What would you have done if you hadn't gone into acting?

ANSWER: If I hadn't pursued acting, I would have been a psychologist. I have always been interested in how the mind works and why people do the things they do. I even use my curiosity about people's motives to break down my characters' personalities, so that I can understand who they are. I begin by building a life for each character before they appear on stage and imagining their life after they exit. This gives me a complete understanding of their emotions and reactions. Through this process, I bring a fully developed, three-dimensional character to life, incorporating my passion for psychology into my "day job."

It is good that I got the job as Thelma because my "first" job in New York only lasted about six hours. I had to convince my dad to let me work, and when I finally did, I called Corvettes, a store across the street that I knew was hiring.

I introduced myself over the phone. "Hello. My name is BernNadette Stanislaus, and I'd like to apply for the job opening."

The man said, "Sure, come on in."

"Okay. I am across the street, so I'll be right over."

I went to the store's office and greeted the man. "I'm BernNadette Stanislaus, and we spoke on the phone. I am here to apply for the job."

He looked at me and quickly stated, "It's filled."

Based on my last name, which is Polish, I guess he assumed I was white. This was the first time I had dealt with that kind of prejudice.

My next job was at Chock full o'Nuts in Manhattan. When I arrived, I told the lady I was there to apply for a job.

She said, "Oh, we've been waiting for you."

Clearly, they were waiting for someone else, but they put me on the register. I'd never touched a register and didn't know where anything was. I didn't know how to ring up taxes with the purchases. I knew *nothing*, yet there I was! It was a mess; do you hear me?

There was one positive element: next to the register sat a tip bowl. Many friendly and generous young men flashed me a smile and dropped fifty cents or a dollar into that bowl. That was a *lot* of money for a tip in the 1970s, the norm being a nickel or dime. The employees split the tips in the bowl at night's end, so it wasn't all mine. However, I am happy to know that I contributed something.

The whole day was a nightmare, and I just knew they would fire me. So, when I went to collect my pay for the day, I quit before they could fire me. They were relieved, and so was I. God knew I would be an actor because I had no other skills then.

QUESTION: Did you study dance at Alvin Ailey?

ANSWER: Yes, I took dance classes at Alvin Ailey in the summers, and during the school year, I studied at various dance studios around the city. I was five when my grandmother enrolled me in a dance school for ballet and tap, and she told my mother to keep me in dance school. That was a promise my mother kept to her mother. Therefore, I was always in a dance school. I eventually developed into a modern jazz dancer and enjoyed interpretive dance.

QUESTION: Why didn't Thelma learn to cook?

ANSWER: Thelma was not interested in cooking. She wanted to become a doctor, and Florida wanted her daughter to focus on her dreams. So, Florida never made Thelma learn how to cook.

QUESTION: How did you keep a straight face in the episodes with Sweet Daddy Willams and Looting Lenny?

ANSWER: It was hard to keep a straight face even though we had watched their work all week in rehearsals. There was always something different when taping live in front of an audience. Therefore, we would still crack up because these two were so hilarious and creative. That was all part of keeping it professional. We rehearsed each show many times, so we got to laugh most of it out before taping.

QUESTION: Years ago, there were rumors that you and Peabo Bryson dated. Was that true?

ANSWER: One day at the studio, I was called to the office for a flower delivery. I arrived at the front desk to the most exquisite miniature peach roses, the tips of which looked like they had been dipped in red paint. I had never seen such beautiful flowers.

The secretary said, "They are from Peabo Bryson."

"I don't know a Peabo Bryson."

The secretary put the phone receiver to her ear and said, "She doesn't know a Peabo Bryson."

Shocked, I realized he had heard what I said. We didn't date, but even to this day, Peabo and I remain good friends, and he still teases me about that. I believe he and I will be friends forever.

QUESTION: What was your favorite episode?
ANSWER: "The Wedding" and "Thelma's African Romance." One of my favorite episodes to film was "Thelma's Wedding. It truly felt like a real wedding to me. I even wore Miss Adella Farmar, our wardrobe mistress's wedding dress, which added a personal touch. Ralph Carter, who played Michael, sang Stevie Wonder's "You and I" beautifully. To top it off, Esther Rolle returned to the show after being absent for a year. Her presence made the episode even more special. It's an experience I will never forget.

Another episode I loved was "Thelma's African Romance." This two-part episode allowed me to showcase African culture's beauty. I enjoyed having my hair braided each week and wearing stunning African outfits. It was a joy to be part of a story celebrating Africa's rich traditions. In the storyline, Ibe, my character's love interest, wanted to marry Thelma but couldn't guarantee she'd be his only wife, as his culture accepted polygamy. For Thelma, a proud all-American girl from the Cabrini-Green projects in Chicago, that just would not work.

QUESTION: What episode do you believe was the best showcase of your acting skills?

ANSWER: "Thelma's African Romance, Part II." Thelma discovers she will not be the prince's only wife in this episode. Thelma's emotional confusion has to be convincing to the audience. I had to communicate my heartbreak about Thelma's relationship with Ibe not working *and* still be strong and stand up for what she believed, so I had to show both at the same time.

QUESTION: Were there any *Good Times* episodes that you were not in?

ANSWER: Yes, there was one episode, and it was the one when Willona had a party after adopting Penny. Penny's mom, played by Chip Fields, appeared at the party, and there was a big fight. I was not in that episode.

QUESTION: Did you go to a lot of Hollywood parties while you were on *Good Times*?

ANSWER: During the 1970s, Hollywood was less populated with entertainers compared to today, and Redd Foxx's house was a popular gathering place. He threw parties almost every weekend, and you knew it would be a good time. His house was up in the hills, and the front area was always full of music, great food, and interesting people. That's where I spent my time. I remember sitting on the couch with Michael

Jackson one night, and we even took pictures together. It was always fun, but there were other areas of the house into which I didn't venture. I never really knew what was happening in the back. I just knew it wasn't where I was supposed to be.

We'd also occasionally go to Richard Pryor's house, which had a similar vibe. It was a beautiful home with lively parties, but I stayed in the front, where I knew I belonged. I enjoyed seeing the entertainers and soaking in the fun atmosphere.

QUESTION: Have you ever met President Obama?

ANSWER: Yes, but then he was Senator Obama. I was on the red carpet at the 2005 NAACP Image Awards. My husband saw him and Michelle right behind us. My husband turned to him and said, "Senator Obama."

That's when then-Senator Obama held his hand up as if to stop us. "We know Thelma. We watch *Good Times*."

QUESTION: Girl, what are you eating, and where is the fountain of youth?

ANSWER: When I moved to California, I jogged daily. I would head down Fountain Avenue, stop at the Catholic Church on the corner, and say my morning prayers before jogging. It became my morning ritual. Until then, dance classes were how I exercised. So, I still jog and eat healthy foods like fish and vegetables. Back then, we did not have personal trainers or nutritionists. It was up to the individual to develop healthy eating and exercise habits. Those early habits serve me well today.

I will let you in on a little secret, though. I may or may not *occasionally* enjoy some hard candy or a green sour apple Blow Pop. Also, if you see my granddaughter and I dipping our fries into a soft-serve ice cream cone at McDonald's—no, you didn't.

QUESTION: When did your daughters realize you were Thelma?

ANSWER: When my daughters were young, they used to sleep in bed with me while the TV was on. One night, *Good Times* was playing, and they heard my voice. They woke me up and excitedly said, "Mom, look!" pointing from the TV to me. I smiled and said, "Yes, that's me on TV." They didn't ask any questions, though; they just responded, "Oh, okay," and went back to sleep.

Fan Encounters and Reactions

QUESTION: How did you feel when you first discovered you were every young boy's first crush, and what was your reaction?

ANSWER: Aside from my fan letters, I realized I was a first crush when I had book signings in 2006. It may sound strange that I did not know before, but they did not have social media back then. Therefore, I could not directly communicate with or respond to my fans like I can today. Book signings allowed me to meet and speak to my fans one-on-one. That was when I heard stories of how they enjoyed Thelma and how she inspired them.

I have heard so many magnificent stories from so many amazing fans. Some women told me how my outfits and hair inspired their look for school the next day. They also shared how my character showed them that a brown-skinned girl could be intelligent, pleasant, *and* bold enough to speak her mind. They informed me I convinced them they could be dancers, doctors, or whatever else they wanted to be. Thelma empowered them to understand they could reach their goals. They said I was their big sister, and I am honored to have been a role model for young girls of every color. Men told me I was their first TV crush when they were young.

My reaction to finding out that I was a first crush truly made me blush because I had never seen myself that way. While working on the show, my goal wasn't to be a first crush but an excellent actress. However, to be considered a first crush produces deep joy and gratitude.

Believe it or not, there is a downside to being a first crush. Coming from my tight-knit community in Brooklyn, navigating personal relationships was a culture shock. I had to learn to discern if someone wanted to date me or form a friendship because I was Thelma on *Good Times* or if they wanted to get to know BernNadette. Like privacy, knowing who's really got your back is a luxury you exchange for being in the spotlight.

QUESTION: Did you get a lot of fan mail?

ANSWER: Yes. We all did. Mine was not always appropriate, as you can imagine. Jimmie, Ralph, and I were on the Sherri Shepherd show, *SHERRI*, for our show's fiftieth anniversary. We played a trivia game where Sherri asked us who-did-what questions. We held pictures of our faces to use as answers. We all held up my picture when she asked who got the most inappropriate fan mail. Sherri asked if I got marriage proposals in the mail. I told her no, but I got a lot of fan mail from inmates. I told her they would "describe things." Never a dull moment.

QUESTION: Do you still get residuals (payments) for reruns?

ANSWER: Yes. I have my mom to thank for that. When the show ended, the cast was asked if we wanted to receive a lump sum to buy out of the show. That meant that we would not get residuals if reruns of the show ran. I remember calling my mother in New York to ask her if I should sign off on the show.

She replied, "I am not there, and your lawyer is not there, so you don't sign a thing."

I returned to the office and said, "No. I won't be signing anything."

Boy, am I glad, too. I had a wise mother. Just look at how many years *Good Times* has been replayed on television. I still get my residuals to this day.

QUESTION: What was your favorite costume of Thelma's for the entire series (other than the wedding dress)?

ANSWER: When I told Larry I wasn't moving to California with him, I wore a denim jacket and bell-bottom jeans. That was my favorite outfit on the show, although I enjoyed wearing a few other outfits, including my lavender halter prom dress.

QUESTION: Were you one of the theme song singers?

ANSWER: No, I was not. Jim Gilstrap and Sondra "Blinky" Williams were the wonderful and talented *Good Times* theme song singers.

QUESTION: Did you ever visit the Cabrini-Green projects in Chicago?

ANSWER: Yes, I visited the Cabrini-Green projects, Thanks to Esther Rolle, who made sure Ralph, Ja'Net, and I were invited to do the Bud Billiken Parade. In fact, we were invited for two years. After the parade the first year, we were escorted to the Cabrini-Green projects. When we got there, we were surrounded by a crowd of wonderful fans. It was an enlightening and inspiring experience.

QUESTION: Thelma was put in many uncomfortable situations. The episode "Willona's Surprise" makes me emotional, and I'm sure it speaks to a lot of people. Is there a backstory to that episode? Were you nervous? Thank you for taking on such a tough subject.

ANSWER: There was no backstory. The creators wanted to address this topic on the show, so they did. Many young women don't know what to do in these situations. It was helpful for them to see that they were not alone and that it wasn't their fault. It was one of the many tough social issues *Good Times* addressed. No, I was not nervous. That was me acting.

QUESTION: Do you feel like Florida held the family back?

ANSWER: No, I do not believe Florida held the family back. I believe she had three children living in a rough neighborhood and was protective of them. Florida was also a very supportive wife to James.

QUESTION: Were those real emotions from you when James died?

ANSWER: Yes, those emotions were very real to me because it felt like our real father was ripped out of the family. It was a sudden shock to discover that James would no longer be a part of our family. So, it was a great loss for me and the show. It intensely impacted us all.

Set and Cast Dynamics

QUESTION: Did everyone in the cast *really* get along with each other?

ANSWER: Yes, we all got along very well. It always felt like magic on Thursdays while taping the show. All of us felt it. We may have had different ages and interests, but it was like family when we came together. This is why I call my cast on *Good Times* my second family.

QUESTION: I loved when you danced to "Native New Yorker" on *Good Times*. How did it come about?

ANSWER: It came about because everyone had a different talent, and we had the opportunity to showcase that talent on this episode of *Good Times*. I chose to dance to Odyssey's Native New Yorker. I am from New York, I choreographed my dance and Adella Farmar our wardrobe mistress helped me to design the outfit I wore. She said it must be something that flows and a bright beautiful color. My dance turned out very enjoyable to perform and I am so glad you loved my dance.

QUESTION: How did you like performing The Supremes' "Stop! In the Name of Love" for the rent party?

ANSWER: I really enjoyed performing The Supremes "Stop! In the Name of Love." Esther, Ja'Net, and I had so much fun practicing, singing, and learning the dance moves.

This was extremely a lot of fun for all of us. I choreographed the dance moves and Adella Farmar (the wardrobe mistress) dressed us so nicely.

QUESTION: Did Janet Jackson show signs of greatness when Thelma, Willona, Florida, and Penny sung and danced to "Steam Heat" as the Pointless Sisters?
ANSWERS: Even though Janet was only twelve years old when we did the Christmas show and rehearsed for it, she never missed a beat. Look at who she turned out to be—go, Ms. Jackson!

QUESTION: Were there any romantic relationships between cast members?
ANSWER: No. We were like family and behaved like one.

QUESTION: Where did that kitchen door next to the stove lead?
ANSWER: The kitchen door was built into the set's wall, so it didn't lead anywhere. It didn't open, and the other side of that door was the back of the set.

QUESTION: Was the audience included during scenes outside of the Evans' home, like when J.J. went to jail?
ANSWER: Yes. Different locations were constructed alongside the apartment on the same soundstage.

QUESTION: Did you rehearse the "Keith smack" heard around the world?
ANSWER: No. That was done live in one take.

QUESTION: Who was your mom's favorite cast member?
ANSWER: Me, of course!

QUESTION: Which cast members didn't want the show to end?
ANSWER: All of us. No one wanted it to end.

QUESTION: Do you all still see each other? If yes, are you all still close?
ANSWER: Yes, we still see each other. Jimmie Walker, Ralph Carter, and I are all still very close, and we call and keep up with each other. We also often do Hollywood book signings together. Although she's quite busy, I still see Janet from time to time. Before John Amos passed, I saw him pretty often, too.

Hollywood Realities and Opportunities

QUESTION: Was the cost of living high in the 1970s?
ANSWER: It wasn't too high in the 1970s. My first apartment was on Fountain Avenue in Hollywood, and it was

a large studio apartment, too. The rent was $150 a month. That same apartment today would cost at least $3,800 a month.

QUESTION: What happened to Keith Anderson?
ANSWER: Ben Powers, who played my husband, Keith, passed away on April 6, 2015, from cancer. All of us genuinely miss him.

QUESTION: What happened to Lenny?
ANSWER: Sadly, Dap "Sugar" Willie, who played Looting Lenny, passed away on October 15, 1994, after a brave fight against lung cancer. He was only fifty-five.

QUESTION: What happened to Michael Moye?
ANSWER: Michael's first writing job was on *Good Times*. He went on to create the sitcom *Married with Children*.

QUESTION: Did Florida and Carl ever get married in Arizona?
ANSWER: Yes, they did.

QUESTION: How hard was it to see the show end? Did you know ahead of time?
ANSWER: It was tough and disappointing. It didn't make sense for it to end because it was still in the top ten. I found out halfway through the last season that it was ending. The show could have continued, or Thelma and Keith could have had a spin-off show.

QUESTION: Why did the show always keep the family down?

ANSWER: There wouldn't have been a show if they hadn't. The show's premise was to accurately portray Black families' struggles in the projects, which is why they "made it" when the show ended.

QUESTION: Did you ever meet Mabel King (Mama Thomas on *What's Happening!*) or Isabel Sanford (Weezy on *The Jeffersons*)?

ANSWER: Yes, I met them, and my dad wanted to meet Sherman Hensley, who played George Jefferson on *The Jeffersons*, so I made sure he did. Sherman Hemsley's walk on the set was exactly how my dad walked in real life.

QUESTION: How come J.J.'s art never made it big?

ANSWER: It did! At the end of the series, J.J. got an offer from a comic company. I was flattered by the fact that they used my image as Dyn-O-Woman.

QUESTION: Have there been any discussions about a reunion show or movie?

ANSWER: Yes. There was even a script. However, we couldn't coordinate our schedules.

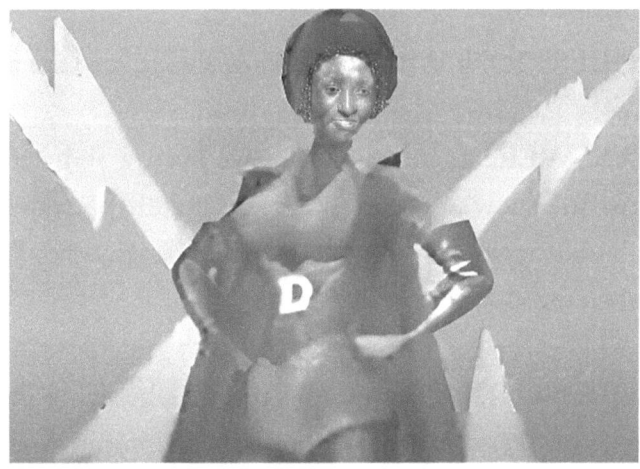

*Dyno-Woman, Good Times,
"The End of the Rainbow" episode.*

QUESTION: How did your life change after the show ended? Did you face challenges transitioning from such a well-known role to new projects?

ANSWER: I had to step out into the real world for the first time and be independent without the support of *Good Times* or my parents. Remember, I came straight from living at home and onto a number-one TV show for *five years*. It felt like I had emerged from a bubble and a time warp and entered reality. I adjusted to a new way of living, and it was an exciting time in my life.

Back then, an actress was an actress. I stayed in California but visited New York every three or four months. I continued to act in plays across the country and taught dance and acting classes. I taught acting at Miles College in Birmingham, Alabama, for a year. Acting is inconsistent work, so there can be downtime between projects. I busied myself with various things, like learning to paint with oil and watercolors. I remember painting a fox's face in watercolor and my mom was watching me.

As I finished the fox's eyes, my mom looked at it and said, "You got him." She meant I had captured the essence of the fox through the eyes. I will always hold her words and the painting of my fox dear to my heart.

QUESTION: Since you were careful about what you ate, did you ever splurge at Roscoe's Chicken & Waffles?

ANSWER: Another experience that highlighted the privilege of celebrity occurred when our cast received an invitation to the opening of the first Roscoe's Chicken & Waffles restaurant in Los Angeles. We taped *Good Times* at KTLA studios on Sunset Boulevard, and Roscoe's was across the street. At the opening, we mingled with celebrities like Phyllis Hyman and Natalie Cole. Forty years after its debut in Hollywood, this chicken and waffle chain has spread across California. I am glad to have been there for its ribbon-cutting ceremony. Every time I pass by or eat there, I remember my first walk through their doors on opening night.

QUESTION: How would Thelma navigate the world today? Would she face the same challenges, or would things be different?

ANSWER: Thelma would have a leadership role. She could be a professor, teaching and sharing her knowledge. She would have some of the same challenges but more of a voice than in the 1970s. There would be more advocacy opportunities, so she would be busy contributing wherever possible to improve the world.

QUESTION: What has it been like revisiting *Good Times* through fan conventions, interviews, or reunions?
ANSWER: I love revisiting *Good Times*. In many ways, it feels like going home.

QUESTION: When are you returning to the screen?
ANSWER: I already have! I play Nee Nee Duncan on Carl Weber's *The Family Business*, a BET original series.

QUESTION: Has the cast of *Good Times* ever won an award?
ANSWER: Yes, we received the TV Land Impact Award in 2006, and it was presented to us by Quentin Tarantino.

CHAPTER 9

Personal Reflections

When I landed the role of Thelma Evans, my life changed instantly. It was December 20, right before Christmas, when I got the call that I had been cast and had just a week to pack up and move to Hollywood by December 27. What started as a role on *Good Times* quickly turned into a life-altering journey—one that brought me more than just fame. It was a blessing that shaped my career, a sense of purpose, and responsibilities.

Being the first African American teenage girl to appear on television regularly came with a weight that I didn't take lightly. My father always stressed the importance of striving for excellence, especially since I was the eldest of five children. His advice rang true on and off the screen—I knew young girls, especially those who looked like me, were watching closely. I felt the weight of the responsibility to show people that whatever stereotypes were out there about Black girls were wrong. I wanted Thelma to be someone they could admire; someone whose actions inspired them. I behaved this way in real life, too.

When I joined the cast, I had a strong drive to ensure Thelma was more than the teenage daughter. I envisioned her as a symbol of hope and ambition for young Black women everywhere. That's what I communicated to the writers, drawing from my upbringing in the Brownsville projects of Brooklyn. I wanted Thelma to be bright, focused, and full of dreams, a character reaching for more. The writers embraced my vision thanks to Esther Rolle's support and advocacy. Her influence wasn't limited to that one change; she was instrumental in pushing for authenticity and representation throughout the industry. Esther wasn't just a co-star—she became my Hollywood mother, guiding me professionally and personally.

Esther helped Thelma find her voice, but I almost lost it. I was in the third year of the show when I noticed that my voice sounded very deep and unnatural. My throat began to hurt when I spoke. In the evenings, it got worse. It hurt to even talk, and at night, I could hardly say any words at all.

I went to see a specialist. The doctor told me I needed an operation to remove polyps from my vocal cords if I wanted to sound normal again. They told me an operation like this went one of two ways: lose my voice forever, or come out just fine, and my voice would return to normal.

Good Times, Ain't We Lucky We Got 'Em:
Memoir of an American Sweetheart

I had the operation, and they told me not to speak for months to allow my vocal cords to heal properly. We relayed this information to the show's producers, and they suggested I learn the script as usual but not speak until tape night. I asked my doctor if that was okay, and he said it was fine. That is how I stayed on the show while my vocal cords healed. That was a terrifying time for me because if the doctor had said I couldn't use my voice just one day a week on tape night, I would have had to leave the show for a while. However, it worked out fine.

Sometimes things happen for reasons we don't know or understand. Right after the operation, I couldn't use my voice. I could only communicate through writing. There was no such thing as text messaging back then, and it would have served a great purpose for me if we'd had texting and Facetime. Since we didn't, and writing everything down with no spell check either, became too much for me to keep up with, so I stopped trying to communicate altogether and became quiet.

During this time of silence, I wrote poetry. I believe it was God's way of directing me toward another creative avenue in my life. During those four months of healing, the words poured out of me. It was as if it came from somewhere deep within. I wrote major pieces and published them in a book titled, *For Men Only*. It was during this time that I became a serious writer, and it was the starting point that inspired me to pen the kind of poetry I write today. God's hand sat me down and quieted me to hear my inner voice. The temporary death of my physical voice gave birth to my writing voice. Here is one of my poems:

Beauty

They say beauty is in the eyes of the beholder,
Well, if it is, then I behold a spirit that soars,
Higher than anyone I've known,
A heart that beats my name,
A mind that connects and yet has mystery.
This person and I have
Mountains and oceans of history.

If beauty is in the eye of the beholder,
Then I behold a quiet, gentleness,
A raging strength,
A desperate desire to be set free.
To be all that he ever imagined he'd be.
If beauty is in the eye of the beholder,
Then let me tell you what I see.

I see my knight in shining armor, waiting for me.
The late-night poetry being sent.
That special look only for me.
The embrace that lets me know,
He is always there.

Good Times, Ain't We Lucky We Got 'Em:
Memoir of an American Sweetheart

That soul connection that creates,
The Eternity of us.

If beauty is in the eye of the beholder,
Then,
Let me just say,
"I behold You"

The impact of *Good Times* was historical and monumental. I saw its impact firsthand through the people who have approached me over the years. Women have told me how Thelma's strength and grace empowered them, how her presence on screen made them feel seen.

Once, a Black woman approached me in public crying and whispered in my ear, "You don't know what you meant to me."

Another time, I met a white woman who wept as she said, "I watched your show as a child experiencing sexual abuse. *Good Times* gave me a healthy, loving family to live vicariously through." She went on to tell me how much she appreciated Penny's story arc about child abuse.

Good Times's storylines had universal themes that reached across all races and cultures. We were a surrogate family for orphans and the abused. We made people laugh during dark days and personal tragedies. We modeled positive ways to interact with family and the community. I cannot stress enough how blessed it was to be a part of something like this.

Esther's legacy lives on through the doors she helped open, and I am honored to have been a part of that movement. My time on *Good Times* wasn't just about acting; it was about making sure that girls like me knew they could aim higher, dream bigger, and break barriers—on screen and off.

CHAPTER 10

A Cultural Impact Beyond the Screen

From the outset of *Good Times*, the significance of being chosen for the show was profound, though its full impact hadn't immediately dawned on me. Yet, even then, I sensed its importance. It wasn't just another acting job but a pioneering moment in television history. *Good Times* stood out as the first show to depict an African American family, complete with a mother, father, and three children—a portrayal that rang true for audiences longing to see themselves reflected on the screen.

For many viewers, *Good Times* was their first glimpse into the realities of Black family life. My father likened it to the first reality TV show because of its striking authenticity. The show's creators, Eric Monte and Michael Evans, drew from their experiences growing up in Cabrini Green to craft genuine and relatable stories. This authenticity was a crucial factor in the show's success.

Under Norman Lear's guidance, the show flourished, challenging stereotypes and presenting characters who felt like real people rather than caricatures. The show tackled issues with nuance and empathy, never shying away from the complexities of life in the inner city.

As years passed, *Good Times* resonated with audiences of all ages. Its timeless lessons on family, love, and resilience have endured through the decades. At book signings and speaking engagements, the stories from fans who credit the show with shaping their understanding of family and community have deeply moved me.

For many viewers, John Amos's portrayal of James Evans was like having a surrogate father on screen, while Ralph Carter's character, Michael Evans, represented a new era of woke representation. It was a privilege to play Thelma Evans, and I feel honored to hear from fans who view her as a sister or a role model.

Good Times wasn't just a TV show—it was a cultural touchstone, a source of comfort and inspiration for millions of viewers. *Good Times* lives on through our loyal and amazing fan base. People have told me they still watch it regularly to experience the nostalgia and familiarity it brings them. Film and music transport people back to who and where they were when they first encountered it. When fans watch the show now, they revisit a profound historical place in time and share a bond with the cast and me. OG fans have introduced

Good Times to their children and grandchildren, sharing their culture and a part of their youth. We were raising America, and our "children" have passed on our lessons, making *Good Times* multigenerational. What a legacy!

As we celebrate our fiftieth anniversary, I'm reminded of the enduring power of storytelling to unite and uplift us, no matter what challenges we face. In a world where representation matters, *Good Times* remains a testament to the importance of authentic storytelling and the enduring impact of diverse voices in the media landscape.

THAT'S A WRAP!

Words of Wisdom for Future Generations

I respect the art of acting. It is truly a skill that one must learn. Acting may look easy as if one could just get up on stage and play a part. On the contrary, acting consistently requires understanding and skill. It was a blessing to have curated a character memorialized as a staple in television history. This rarely happens for an actor on their first show, but I am proof that it *can* happen.

To succeed in the entertainment business, one must wholeheartedly commit themselves. To be in this business, one must have devotion to the personal goal they envisioned because it takes genuine desire, which is often difficult. I am saying this because you will hear "No" more than you will hear "Yes." You must not have, as we call it in the business, "thin skin," which means you must not allow negative feedback to discourage you. Instead, you must develop "thick skin," the inner strength to forge ahead until you reach your goal.

To young people entering this business, you must navigate your acting career with dignity, strength, and humble confidence. Preparation for your audition is critical, so know the character you are reading for, understand why the character is saying the words they are saying, and *memorize your lines*. This will help your dialogue flow much easier.

Here are a few things to remember: You only pay ten percent to the agent when you get the job. You are there to read for a part and are not required, *under* any circumstances, to compromise your morals or integrity to land the part. The ideal job is with a certified and union-bonded company because they must follow the rules of the Screen Actors Guild or AFTRA. Therefore, those jobs seem to be the safest for actors.

Pro tip: Once you finish an audition, try to let it go until you hear the results. If you did your best while auditioning, that is all you can do. Therefore, have faith in your work and don't worry about it anymore.

What Would I Tell the Younger Version of Me?

I would tell my younger self, entering the world of Hollywood, that I am glad I came from a neighborhood that taught me to be resilient. I was prepared for the hard knocks from growing up in a tough neighborhood. What Hollywood presented to me did not surprise or frighten me. I knew if I could make it in Brownsville, Brooklyn, New York, I could make it anywhere.

I would tell my younger self how proud I am of her and how committed she was to herself and her career. I'd also say that I am glad she kept our desire to develop and learn new things along our career journey because I became a poet, author, and painter. Those became my passions in between acting jobs. I have always believed that as we move through life in any career, we must continue growing and learning more of who we are through our desires to learn more of our talents.

As I look back at where I started in the 1970s to where I am now in 2024, I am so proud of women's progress and how far we have come. From me being the first Black female teenager ever on television to Vice President Kamala Harris today, I would say we have come a long way. I am overjoyed to be alive to see this happen in the United States of America.

About BernNadette Stanis

BernNadette Stanis is best known as the quick-witted, savvy, original "It" girl, Thelma Evans, from the groundbreaking sitcom *Good Times*. She was the first African American female teenager to be cast in a full family show, and she remains the personification of the "gem" that young girls aspire to be.

BernNadette's place in television history was solidified by her undeniable contributions to redefining the role of a young Black girl from inner-city ghettos across America, challenging the stereotypes held by the masses. The character Thelma showed that a girl from Chicago's inner-city projects could live a life full of hopes and dreams, while also possessing intelligence, self-respect, dignity, and grace. For BernNadette Stanis, these traits are not just part of a role—they are an intrinsic part of who she is.

The legendary actress and author continues her stellar career, currently starring as Nee Nee Duncan on Carl Weber's *The Family Business* and *The Family Business: New Orleans*.

Captured Moments
My Life in Pictures

BernNadette Stanis with Brittany Rose

Good Times

Good Times, Ain't We Lucky We Got 'Em:
Memoir of an American Sweetheart

Good Times, Ain't We Lucky We Got 'Em: Memoir of an American Sweetheart

Good Times, Ain't We Lucky We Got 'Em:
Memoir of an American Sweetheart

Good Times, Ain't We Lucky We Got 'Em: Memoir of an American Sweetheart

Good Times, Ain't We Lucky We Got 'Em:
Memoir of an American Sweetheart

BernNadette Stanis with Brittany Rose

BernNadette

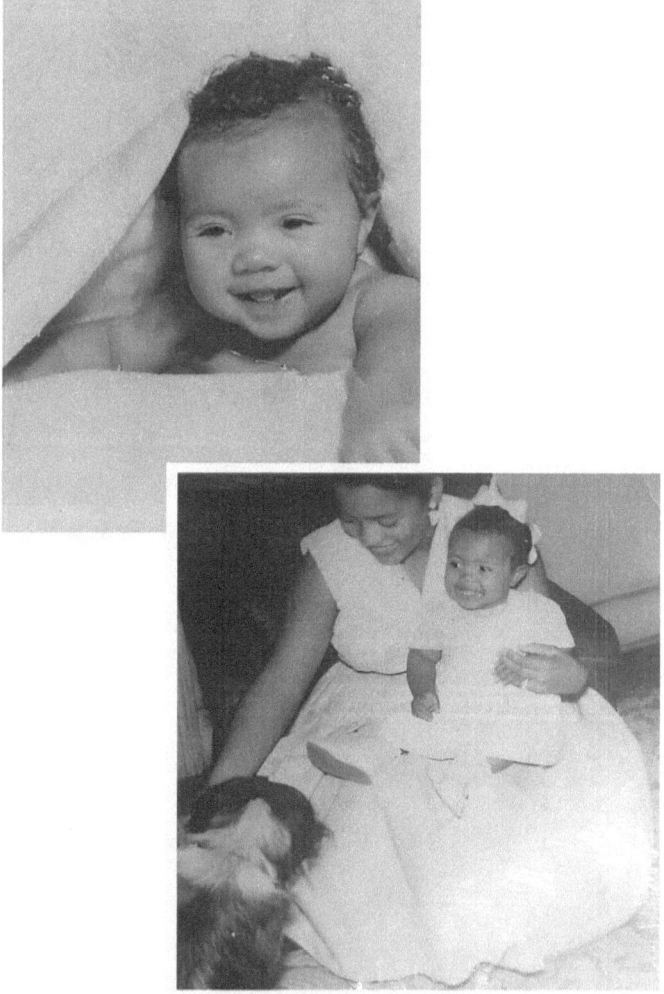

*Baby BernNadette with
her mother, Eula Stanislaus*

Good Times, Ain't We Lucky We Got 'Em:
Memoir of an American Sweetheart

Good Times, Ain't We Lucky We Got 'Em:
Memoir of an American Sweetheart

With my dad.

With Norman Lear and Ja'Net DuBois

BernNadette Stanis with Brittany Rose

With Norman Lear

With Mayor Tom Bradley, Los Angeles, California

Good Times, Ain't We Lucky We Got 'Em: Memoir of an American Sweetheart

BernNadette Stanis with Brittany Rose

Good Times, Ain't We Lucky We Got 'Em:
Memoir of an American Sweetheart

Good Times, Ain't We Lucky We Got 'Em: Memoir of an American Sweetheart

Good Times, Ain't We Lucky We Got 'Em: Memoir of an American Sweetheart

BernNadette Stanis

BernNadette Stanis with Brittany Rose

Good Times, Ain't We Lucky We Got 'Em: Memoir of an American Sweetheart

HALLOWEEN TREAT

Television star BernNadette Stanis is a sweet treat that ought to come in every candy bag this Halloween.

Isaac Sutton

Good Times, Ain't We Lucky We Got 'Em:
Memoir of an American Sweetheart

BernNadette Stanis with Brittany Rose

Good Times, Ain't We Lucky We Got 'Em:
Memoir of an American Sweetheart

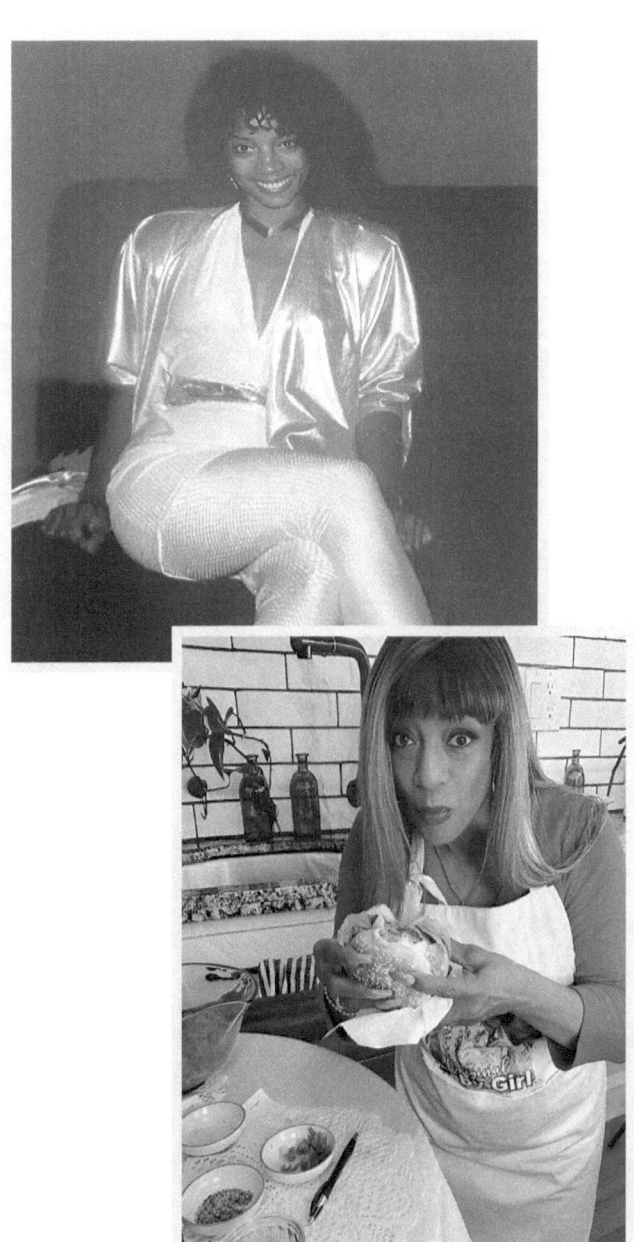

Good Times, Ain't We Lucky We Got 'Em:
Memoir of an American Sweetheart

BernNadette Stanis with Brittany Rose

Good Times, Ain't We Lucky We Got 'Em:
Memoir of an American Sweetheart

Portraying
Nee Nee Duncan
on Carl Weber's
The *Family
Business*

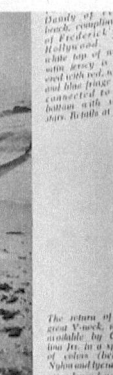

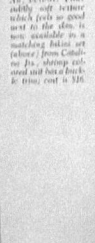

Good Times, Ain't We Lucky We Got 'Em:
Memoir of an American Sweetheart

BernNadette Stanis with Brittany Rose

Good Times, Ain't We Lucky We Got 'Em:
Memoir of an American Sweetheart

BernNadette Stanis with Brittany Rose

Good Times, Ain't We Lucky We Got 'Em:
Memoir of an American Sweetheart

Family

*With
Kevin Fontana*

*With my daughter,
Dior Ravel*

My daughter, Dior.

My daughter, Brittany

Good Times, Ain't We Lucky We Got 'Em: Memoir of an American Sweetheart

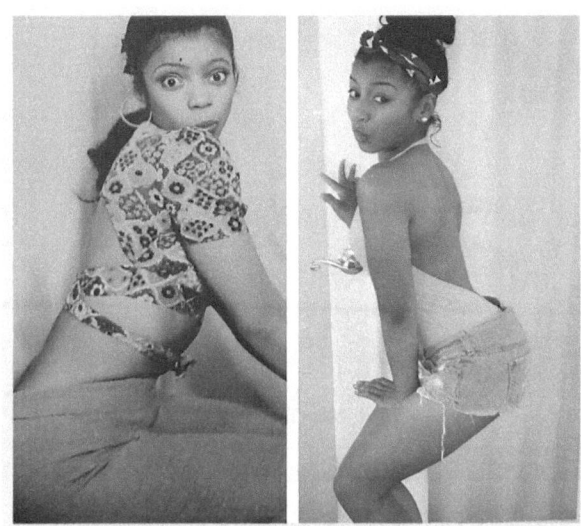

Mirror Image: BernNadette on the left, Brittany on the Right.

(L to R): Young BernNadette, Brittany, Dior

Good Times, Ain't We Lucky We Got 'Em:
Memoir of an American Sweetheart

*My granddaughter,
Leto Manon*

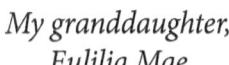

*My granddaughter,
Eulilia Mae*

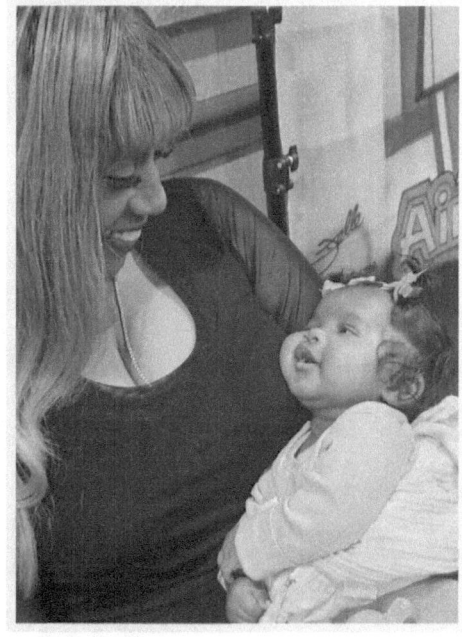

BernNadette Stanis with Brittany Rose

Good Times, Ain't We Lucky We Got 'Em:
Memoir of an American Sweetheart

With my granddaughter, Leto Manon

With my beautiful mother, Eula.

Sade, the Yorkie

With grandaughter, Leto Manon

Good Times, Ain't We Lucky We Got 'Em:
Memoir of an American Sweetheart

Dior and Jimmie Walker

BernNadette Stanis with Brittany Rose

Celebrity Life

With Isaiah Thomas

With
Lawrence Taylor

Good Times, Ain't We Lucky We Got 'Em:
Memoir of an American Sweetheart

*With
Mayor Van R.
Johnson of
Savannah, Georgia*

*With
Gene Chandler*

BernNadette Stanis with Brittany Rose

With Jimmie Walker and Freda Payne

With Ted Lange

Good Times, Ain't We Lucky We Got 'Em:
Memoir of an American Sweetheart

*With Quincy Jones,
Marla Gibbs, and
Anthony Anderson*

*With Ralph Carter
and
Catherine Bach*

With Marla Gibbs

With Ja'Net DuBois, Ralph Carter, Jimmie Walker, and Johnny Brown

Good Times, Ain't We Lucky We Got 'Em:
Memoir of an American Sweetheart

With LeVar Burton and Janet Jackson

With Lisa Ray McCoy and Howard Hewitt

BernNadette Stanis with Brittany Rose

With Pam Grier and Freda Payne

With castmates from Carl Weber's The Family Business: Ben Stephens and Mayirah Teshali

Good Times, Ain't We Lucky We Got 'Em:
Memoir of an American Sweetheart

With Denzel Washington

With Valerie Pettiford, castmate from
Carl Weber's The Famioy Business

Brittany with Rev. Al Sharpton

With Stan Shaw, castmate from Carl Weber's The Family Business

Good Times, Ain't We Lucky We Got 'Em:
Memoir of an American Sweetheart

*With
DJ Jazzy Jeff
and
Will Smith*

With Cicely Tyson

BernNadette Stanis with Brittany Rose

With Ruby Dee

With John Witherspoon and Charlie Murphy on the set of Black Jesus

Good Times, Ain't We Lucky We Got 'Em:
Memoir of an American Sweetheart

With Patti LaBelle

With Jimmy Kimmel

With Jamie Foxx

With Anthony Anderson

Good Times, Ain't We Lucky We Got 'Em:
Memoir of an American Sweetheart

With Woody Harrelson

With Norman Lear, Jimmie Walker, and Ja'Net Dubois

With Ja'Net DuBois, Jimmie Walker, and John Amos

With John Singleton

Good Times, Ain't We Lucky We Got 'Em:
Memoir of an American Sweetheart

With Dominique Wilkins

With Julius "Dr. J." Irving and Brittany

With Ted Lange

With Barbara Eden

Good Times, Ain't We Lucky We Got 'Em: Memoir of an American Sweetheart

With Brittany and Rodney Perry

With Frankie Beverly

With Idris Elba

With Shelly Garrett

Good Times, Ain't We Lucky We Got 'Em:
Memoir of an American Sweetheart

With Bobby Brown

With Mark Eaton

BernNadette Stanis with Brittany Rose

*With
Norm Nixon*

*With
Ralph Sampson*

Good Times, Ain't We Lucky We Got 'Em:
Memoir of an American Sweetheart

With Michael Cooper

With Dominique Wilkins and Bo Kimble

With Rain Pryor

With Larenz Tate

Good Times, Ain't We Lucky We Got 'Em:
Memoir of an American Sweetheart

With Wanda Durant

With
Cuba Gooding, Sr.

BernNadette Stanis with Brittany Rose

With Tom Joyner

With Tommy Ford

Good Times, Ain't We Lucky We Got 'Em:
Memoir of an American Sweetheart

With Wanya Morris, Shawn Stockman, and Nathan Morris of Boyz II Men

With El DeBarge

With Babyface

With Jermaine Jackson, Tito Jackson,
Marlon Jackson, and Jackie Jackson

Good Times, Ain't We Lucky We Got 'Em:
Memoir of an American Sweetheart

With Beyoncé and Brittany

With Dorien Wilson

Script

"Thelma Moves Out"

Season 5
Episode: #0506
Taped: September 8, 1977
Air Date: October 12, 1977

Written by
Michael S. Baser and Kim Weiskopf

Directed by
Gerren Keith

This is BernNadette's original script!

FINAL DRAFT
9/6/77

GOOD TIMES

"Thelma Moves Out"

Executive Producers
Austin and Irma Kalish

Producers
Lloyd Turner
&
Gordon Mitchell

Director
Gerren Keith

Written by
Kim Weiskopf
&
Michael Baser

A
BUD YORKIN-NORMAN LEAR
TANDEM PRODUCTION

EPISODE: #0506
TAPE : 9/8/77
AIR : TBA

GOOD TIMES - #0506

TENTATIVE REHEARSAL & TAPING SCHEDULE

WEDNESDAY, SEPTEMBER 7, 1977   STAGE #7

 ESU & DRY BLOCK/CAMERA BLOCK   9:00 AM - 1:00 PM
 LUNCH   1:00 PM - 2:00 PM
 CAMERA BLOCK   2:00 PM - 4:30 PM
 RUN THRU   4:30 PM - 5:00 PM
 CREW WRAP & CAST NOTES   5:00 PM -

THURSDAY, SEPTEMBER 8, 1977   STAGE #7

 DIRECTOR NOTES W/CAST   1:00 PM - 2:30 PM
 ESU   1:30 PM - 2:30 PM
 FAX   2:30 PM - 4:30 PM
 RUN THRU   4:00 PM -
 CAST NOTES, MAKEUP & WARDROBE   4:30 PM - 5:30 PM
 2 VTR/FAX (DRESS W/AUDIENCE)   5:30 PM - 6:30 PM
 MEAL BREAK & NOTES (In Reh. Hall)   6:30 PM - 7:30 PM
 VT CHECK IN   7:30 PM - 8:00 PM
 2 VTR/FAX (AIR W/AUDIENCE)   8:00 PM - 9:00 PM
 PICK-UPS   9:00 PM -

11:15 - Make Up + Hair being (her in)

Good Times, Ain't We Lucky We Got 'Em:
Memoir of an American Sweetheart

GOOD TIMES

"Thelma Moves Out"

#0506

CAST

```
WILLONA..............................JA'NET DU BOIS
JAMES JUNIOR.........................JIMMIE WALKER
THELMA...............................BERN NADETTE STANIS
MICHAEL..............................RALPH CARTER
PENNY................................JANET JACKSON
BOOKMAN..............................JOHNNY BROWN
PAUL.................................HILLY HICKS
ALVIN................................BOBBY ELLERBEE
KAREN CLAY...........................YAHEE  Yakee
BEAR.................................WILLIAM J. QUINN
```

SETS

EVANS' APARTMENT - HALLWAY

INT. EVANS' APARTMENT

INT. THELMA'S APARTMENT

BernNadette Stanis with Brittany Rose

SHOW OPENING

GOOD TIMES #0506   VTR: 9/8/77

(EXTERIOR SHOTS)

MATTE TITLES

        GOOD TIMES

        Starring

        JA'NET DU BOIS

        RALPH CARTER

        BERN NADETTE STANIS

        with

        JOHNNY BROWN

        JANET JACKSON

        And also starring

        JIMMIE WALKER

        as J.J.

        Executive Producers

        AUSTIN AND IRMA KALISH

        Produced by

        LLOYD TURNER & GORDON MITCHELL

        Created by

        ERIC MONTE

          &

        MICHAEL EVANS

        Developed by

        NORMAN LEAR

Good Times, Ain't We Lucky We Got 'Em:
Memoir of an American Sweetheart

```
                          RUNDOWN
    "GOOD TIMES" #0506   VTR: 9/8/77  AIR:  TBA   KTTV-Studio #7
```

		1	2	3	4
1. SHOW OPENING					
a. OPENING TITLES					
2. COMMERCIAL #1		1:03		1:03	
a. SCENE ONE	(1)				
b. SCENE TWO	(14)				
c. SCENE THREE	(21)				
4. COMMERCIAL #2		1:03		1:03	
5. ACT TWO					
a. SCENE ONE	(22)				
b. SCENE TWO	(29)				
c. SCENE THREE	(35)				
6. END CREDITS					
7. COMMERCIAL #3		1:03		1:03	
8. BUMPER		:03		:03	
9. PROMO		:22		:22	
10. CLOSING/CREDITS					

ACT ONE

SCENE ONE

FADE IN:

INT. EVANS APT. HALLWAY - NIGHT

(THE ELEVATOR DOORS OPEN AND THELMA AND HER DATE, PAUL, COME OUT -- THEY'RE CROSSING TO THE EVAN'S DOORWAY)

THELMA

...Thanks for dinner, Paul.

(TURNS TO HIM)

I just love Chinese food.

(THEY STOP AT DOOR)

PAUL

I sure got lucky with my fortune cookie. I'm going to have this framed.

(TAKES SLIP FROM POCKET AND READS)

"He who reaches out will attain passionate romance..."

THELMA

But remember. Mine said: "He who reaches out will attain fat lip..."

(THEY LAUGH)

Would you like to come in, Paul?

PAUL

Are you sure we won't wake anyone?

THELMA

We have the living room to ourselves.

(THELMA OPENS THE DOOR AND THEY ENTER)

INT. EVANS LIVING ROOM-NIGHT

(AS THEY ENTER, THE ROOM IS IN DARKNESS)

THELMA (CONT'D)

(CROSSES UPSTAGE TO TURN ON LIGHT)

Just a minute. I'll turn on the light.   *Keep ad libing*

PAUL

Keep talking. I'll follow your voice.

THELMA

You're getting warmer.

PAUL

Is this warm enough, Cupcake?

(PAUL TRIPS AND FALLS ON THE BED. AD LIB SOUND OF YELLING AND CONFUSION)

~~J.J.~~

~~Warm nothing. You're hurrying up.~~

(THE LIGHTS COME ON. PAUL IS ON THE SOFA BED, TANGLED UP WITH J.J., WHO HAS BEEN ASLEEP THERE WITH MICHAEL)

THELMA

(CROSSING DOWN TO SOFA)

J.J.! What are you doing here?

PAUL

Who are you?

J.J.

I'm Cupcake. Who are you?

MICHAEL
(SITTING UP)

    What's going on?

PAUL

    Who's that?

MICHAEL

    Who are you?

THELMA

    These are my brothers.

PAUL
(GETTING OUT OF BED)

    Thelma, you told me...

(CROSSES TO GREEN CHAIR)

THELMA

    J.J., Michael, what are you doing out here?

MICHAEL

    Not sleeping, that's for sure.

(RISES--PULLS BLANKET OFF THE BED--EXITS TO BEDROOM)

J.J.
(SITS UP)

    Hey! Come back here with the blanket.
    I feel like a naked chicken!

THELMA

    Well, chicken, here's your feathers!

(THELMA HITS J.J. OVER THE HEAD WITH A PILLOW)

J.J.
(SITS UP)

    Hey! What's wrong with you, girl?

THELMA

You and Michael have your own room now. Why aren't you in it?

J.J.

Because Penny's in there sleep. Willona asked us to baby sit.

THELMA

Why didn't you let her sleep in my room?

J.J.

Thelma, these are Penny's formative years. If she woke up and the first thing she saw was your face it could ruin her for life.

PAUL

(MOVES TO GO)

Maybe I better leave.

THELMA

(CROSSING TO PAUL)

Paul, wait a minute.

J.J.

(CROSSING TO PAUL)

Yeah, bro, no need to rush off. You know it does my heart good to see two young people in love.

(PUTTING HIS ARM AROUND PAUL'S SHOULDER)

Paul, welcome to the family!

THELMA

J.J., what are you talking about?

J.J.

I just want to be sure that Paul's intentions are honorable.

PAUL

It's only our first date!

J.J.

So that's your game! Luring sweet innocent girls to their own apartments. Love 'em and leave 'em.

PAUL

Do you think I'd do something like that to Thelma.

J.J.

Oh, so she's not good enough for you, huh?

PAUL

Thelma?...

THELMA

Maybe you'd better leave, Paul. Will you call?

PAUL

Would you?

(HE EXITS. J.J. CROSSES AND SLAMS THE DOOR)

THELMA

J.J., are you crazy? This is the third time you've pulled a stunt like that since Ma's away.

Good Times, Ain't We Lucky We Got 'Em:
Memoir of an American Sweetheart

```
                    J.J.
    (MOVING BEHIND SOFA LEFT)
        You're better off. Take it from me.
        This one was all hands.
SFX: KNOCK ON DOOR
    (PENNY ENTERS FROM BEDROOM)
                    THELMA
        Look, J.J., from now on mind your own
        business. You're not my father!
SFX: KNOCK ON DOOR
                    PENNY
        Isn't anyone going to answer the door?
                    J.J.
        Now look what you done done. You
        woke Penny up.
                    THELMA
        I woke her? Look J.J., you started this.
        You're Invading my privacy.
                    J.J.
        You're invading the planet, Martian face!
SFX: KNOCK ON DOOR
    (J.J. CROSSES AND OPENS DOOR - IT'S BOOKMAN
    WEARING A LONG NIGHTSHIRT, MATCHING NIGHT CAP AND
    HIS TOOLBELT)
        Speaking of invasions...look what just
        landed. An outer space buffalo.
                    BOOKMAN
        Very funny.
                    (MORE)
```

BOOKMAN (CONT'D)

Look, the neighbors are complaining about the noise coming from this apartment. They can't sleep. And when they can't sleep they call me, so I can't sleep. And when I can't sleep, Mrs. Bookman can't sleep. And when Mrs. Bookman can't sleep...she's mean. And when I say mean, I mean mean like mean Joe Green.

PENNY

(CROSSING BEHIND SOFA LEFT)

Does Mrs. Bookman know you're wearing her clothes?

BOOKMAN

Hey, what's going on here?

THELMA

(CROSSING TO J.J.)

Bookman, this is a family matter and it doesn't concern you, so butt out.

J.J.

Thelma, let the head of the house handle this. Bookman is no ordinary janitor. He is a gentleman and a scholar and deserves to be treated accordingly...Butt out, Rhino Rump!...

(PUSHES BOOKMAN OUT--HE CLOSES DOOR THEN TURNS TO THELMA)

(MORE)

                    J.J. (CONT'D)
    You see, Thelma, it's not what you say,
    it's how you say it.
(CROSSES AROUND THELMA)
    Lucky for us Ma left me in charge.
                    THELMA
    That's news to me... etc.
(J.J. AND THELMA HASSLE)
                    PENNY
    Quiet!
(THEY QUIET)
    Michael's trying to sleep.
(ENTER WILLONA)
                    WILLONA
(CROSSING TO THELMA)
    Hi, Thelma. Sorry I'm late, but we
    were taking inventory and we kept
    coming up with one extra coat. It took
    me two hours before I realized it was
    mine...
(SEES PENNY)
    Penny! What are you doing up at this
    hour?

PENNY

Well...I was asleep, but then Thelma came home with her boyfriend and he ended up in bed with J.J. who he called cupcake which made Thelma throw a pillow at J.J. because he and Michael were supposed to sleep in her room tonight... Then J.J. threw the boyfriend out and that made Thelma real mad at J.J. because he's not her father and then Rhino Rump came in mad cause he's married to mean Joe Green, and that's the name of that tune.

J.J.
(CROSSING TO WILLONA)

Uh,...let me explain. You see, as head of the house--

THELMA

As head of nothin', J.J. I'm fed-up with the way you're trying to run things around here!

J.J.

Me? What have I done wrong?

THELMA

First of all You've been screening my boy friends! Telling me how to live my life! Complaining about my cooking--and Strutting around like some aunt peacock and you just making things miserable for me!

J.J.

Yeah, but what have I done <u>wrong?</u>

WILLONA

Kids, couldn't we talk about this in the morning...

THELMA

J.J., you've got to stop bossing me around!

J.J.

I'm the oldest. Ma left me in charge and if you don't like it, you know what you can do.

THELMA

You're right! ~~I'm leaving!~~ I don't know what I can do about it. I'm moving out!
(CROSSING UPSTAGE LEFT--J.J. FOLLOWS)

J.J.

You can't do that!
(THEY HASSLE)

WILLONA

(CROSSING TO PENNY--TO J.J. AND THELMA)

Hold it! Hold it!
(MOVING PENNY TO DOOR)

Penny, you get home and into bed.
(SHE GIVES HER KEY)

Here's the key.

PENNY

Aw, Willona, do I have to?

                    WILLONA

    You can watch T.V. until I get there.

                    PENNY

(TURNS TO THELMA AND J.J.)

    But this is better than T.V.

                    WILLONA

    Go on now.

(EXIT PENNY--CROSSING TO J.J.)

    All right, Thelma, now that Penny's
    gone...

                    J.J.

    Pardon moi. I have more important
    things to attend to.

(CROSSES BELOW THELMA TO THE BATHROOM)

                    WILLONA

    ...What's all this about you movin' out?

                    THELMA

    Willona, it's the only answer.

                    WILLONA

    Come on, girl. J.J. may be hot dog on
    the outside, but inside he's all mush...

                    THELMA

    I've been saying that about his brain
    for years...

(THELMA CROSSES TO THE BATHROOM, FINDS THE
DOOR LOCKED)

    J.J., come out of there!

Good Times, Ain't We Lucky We Got 'Em:
Memoir of an American Sweetheart

            J.J.

  Does the King come out of his castle?

            THELMA

(TO WILLONA)

  See what I mean?

(THELMA STALKS OFF TO HER BEDROOM. J.J.
COMES OUT OF THE BATHROOM)

            J.J.

(CROSSING TO WILLONA)

  Has Hurricane Thelma blown over?

            WILLONA

  All clear, you can get back to your

  room now. Where is Gramps?

            THELMA (O.S.)

  Get out of my bed!

(ENTER THELMA WITH A SLEEPY MICHAEL IN
TOW--HE CARRIES A BLANKET)

            MICHAEL

  Doesn't anybody ever sleep in this house?

(EXITS INTO BATHROOM)

            WILLONA

  That's a good idea. Why don't we all go

  to sleep. We'll talk about it in the

  morning, okay?

            THELMA

  Okay, I'll go to sleep, and we'll talk about

  it in the morning.

WILLONA

Good!

~~THELMA~~
~~(And then I'll move out!)~~   Thelma
                                 And Then I'm
(THELMA EXITS TO HER BEDROOM AND SLAMS THE   Moving Out
DOOR. AS WE:)

DISSOLVE TO:

ACT ONE

SCENE TWO

INT. EVANS APT-MORNING

(MICHAEL DRINKS A GLASS OF JUICE--GLANCES OVER J.J.'S SHOULDER LOOKING THROUGH A MAGAZINE)

     J.J.

Michael, my man, notice the treatment of light and dark shades in a pictorial work of art. In the ad business we call this technique.

     MICHAEL

In the vice squad they call it pornography.

(ENTER WILLONA)

     WILLONA

(CROSSING TO J.J.)

Hi, everybody. How's it going?

     J.J.

(STILL LOOKING AT MAGAZINE)

Real fine.

     WILLONA

Where's Thelma?

     MICHAEL

Still sleeping.

     WILLONA

This late?

(SHE CROSSES TO THELMA'S DOOR)

                THELMA
            You do?

                WILLONA
            But on the other hand, you're still
            young, and you've got plenty of time.
                MICHAEL
            (CROSSING BELOW J.J.)
            Right.

                WILLONA
            (MOVING TOWARDS MICHAEL--THELMA FOLLOWS)
            Then again, on the other hand, kids
            grow up quicker these days.
                THELMA
            Exactly.

                WILLONA
            (TURNS TO THELMA)
            But on the other hand, you have certain
            obligations to your family...
                J.J.
            Hear! Hear!

                WILLONA
            (TAKES A FEW STEPS TOWARD J.J.)
            Then again, on the other hand. Thelma
            needs space. She needs the freedom to
            grow.
                THELMA
            Amen.

                    WILLONA
(CROSSING TO THELMA)
    But on the other hand--

                    J.J.
    Willona, you got more hands than that
    turkey Thelma brought home last night.

                    THELMA
(CROSSING TO J.J.)
    Get off my case, J.J.!...
(CROSSES TO WILLONA)
    Come on, Willona, what do you honestly
    think?

                    WILLONA
    I honestly think that you're old enough
    to make your own decisions. And if you
    feel you need a place of your own--God
    bless!

                    THELMA
    Oh, thank you, Willona!
(HUGS HER)

                    WILLONA
    But on the other hand--

                    THELMA
    Willona!

                    WILLONA
(SHE AND THELMA MOVE BEHIND MID SOFA)
    Come on. I'll help you look for a place.

THELMA

You're too late. I already found an apartment.

WILLONA

You what? So that's where you were this morning!

J.J.

(CROSSING TO THELMA)

As the designated chief executive of this family, I am afraid I will have to veto this decision on the grounds that letting Thelma loose on mankind would constitute cruel and unusual punishment.

WILLONA

Overruled!

(J.J. CROSSES TO GREEN CHAIR)

MICHAEL

(CROSSING TO THELMA)

Hey, Thelma, what's your place like?

THELMA

It's perfect. It's near campus, I can walk to school, one of my roommates is a girl I know from dance class and my share of the rent is only fifty dollars.

WILLONA

Sounds reasonable. How soon do you move in? The first of the month?

THELMA

I'm moving in today.

Good Times, Ain't We Lucky We Got 'Em: Memoir of an American Sweetheart

J.J.

Uh, Thelma...what's the rush?

THELMA

(CROSSING TO J.J.)

I thought you couldn't wait to get rid of me.

J.J.

Yeah, I know, it's just that...what I mean is...hey, look around. There's just the three of us now. It's not like I thought we'd stay together forever... I knew we'd some day go our separate ways. Me to become an executive on Madison Avenue...Michael to become a Justice of the Supreme Court and you, Thelma, to become a model...poster girl for the American Kennel Club.

(THELMA MOVES TO GO - J.J. STOPS HER)

What I'm trying to say is, I'm going to miss you girl.

THELMA

Oh, J.J., I'll miss you, too.

(CROSSING BETWEEN WILLONA AND MICHAEL)

All of you...

(CROSSING TO WILLONA)

You know, Willona, you're so Lucky. It's going to be so Easy 'Cause for you to let go when Penny wants to move out.

                    WILLONA
            Penny? No way. She'll be living with
            me till her first wedding anniversary.
            Then she and her husband can both move out.
    (THEY LAUGH AS WE:)
    DISSOLVE TO:

ACT ONE

SCENE THREE

INT. HALLWAY OUTSIDE THELMA'S APARTMENT - DAY

(A LITTLE LATER. THELMA IS BURSTING WITH EXCITEMENT. WILLONA IS WINDED FROM THE LONG CLIMB UP THE STAIRS - THEY CROSS TO DOOR)

THELMA

Well, this is it. What do you think?

WILLONA

It reminds me of home. The elevator doesn't work.

(THELMA KNOCKS ON THE DOOR)

THELMA

Wait till you see the inside.

(THE DOOR OPENS, A YOUNG BLACK MAN, ALVIN, STANDS THERE - WEARING ONLY BOXER SHORTS)

WILLONA

Oh! Sorry. We must have the wrong apartment.

(MOVES TO GO)

THELMA

(STOPPING HER)

Willona. ~~This is the right apartment.~~ this is Alvin... one of my roommates.

(WILLONA LOOKS ALVIN UP AND DOWN AND UP AGAIN AS WE:)

FADE OUT:

END OF ACT ONE

ACT TWO

SCENE ONE

FADE IN:

INT. THELMA'S APARTMENT - DAY

(CONTINUOUS ACTION. AN APARTMENT WITH KITCHEN, TWO O.S. BEDROOMS AND A BATHROOM... EVERYTHING IS SMALL, CRAMPED, AND CLUTTERED. THERE IS A BULKY, CRUMPLED SLEEPING BAG ON THE SOFA. THELMA AND WILLONA ENTER - THEY CROSS DOWN STAGE PAST SOFA LEFT)

THELMA

Alvin, I'd like you to meet Willona Woods, a friend.

ALVIN

Hi.

WILLONA

(LOOKING AT HIS BRIEF ATTIRE)

I hope you're going jogging.

(ALVIN EXITS TO BEDROOM)

WILLONA

Thelma, you didn't mention that one of your roommates was a man.

THELMA

Willona, I grew up in the same house with two brothers. What's the difference?

WILLONA

Oh, there's a difference, all right.

(KAREN ENTERS FROM OTHER BEDROOM)

23.

~~KAREN~~
(CROSSING TO WILLONA)

~~Mrs. Evans, how marvelous to see you.~~
(SHE HUGS WILLONA)

You look just like your daughter.

THELMA

Uh, Karen, this is Willona Woods, a ~~good~~ friend. *I'd like you to meet... Mrs. Evans*

KAREN

~~Oh... Well, I was just trying to be polite.~~ *Whatever...*

THELMA

This is my rommate, Karen Clay.
(ENTER J.J., PUFFING, CARRYING BOXES)

J.J.

Hey Thelma, where do you want...
(MOVES TO KAREN)

Well, well, well.
(DROPS BOXES)

Thelma dear, you didn't tell me the apartment came with such delectable built-ins.

THELMA

The clarinet with feet is my brother. J.J., this is Karen.
(J.J. TAKES KAREN'S HAND AND PLANTS A KISS UPON IT)

J.J.

Enchanté, senorita.

                        THELMA

            Come on, Willona. I'll show you around.
(THEY CROSS UPSTAGE)

                        WILLONA

            Do I really look old enough to be your
            mother?

                        J.J.

            Le grand tour. Good idea. Take your
            time.
(THELMA AND WILLONA EXIT TO BEDROOMS)

            I suppose Thelma's told you that I am
            an arteest. Painting is my game and
            advertising is my claim to fame.

                        KAREN

            Do you have your own studio?

                        J.J.

            No, I gave up my garret for a position
            in advertising.

                        KAREN
(PUSHING J.J. TOWARDS DESK)

            Sell out! I bet you enjoy duping the
            masses into buying worthless garbage
            they can't use or afford. People like
            you should be put up against a wall
            and shot.

                        J.J.

            Hey, lady, I just draw pictures.
(THELMA AND WILLONA RE-ENTER - THEY CROSS DOWN
TO SOFA RIGHT)

                        THELMA

    Willona, what do you think of the place?

(WILLONA HAS MOVED IN FRONT OF MID-SOFA)

                        WILLONA

    Well it's....cozy.

(SHE SITS ON THE COUCH. THEN LEAPS TO HER
FEET WHEN BEAR STEPS OUT OF THE SLEEPING BAG)

                        KAREN

(CROSSING TO BEAR)

        This is Bear...our other roommate.

                        BEAR

(RISING)

        Hi. Glad to meet you!

(HE SHAKES WILLONA'S HAND VIGOROUSLY)

                        THELMA

    Willona, I know what you're thinking--

                        WILLONA

        I'm thinking I may never use this hand
        again...

(MOVING THELMA DOWNSTAGE)

        Thelma, if you and Karen share one
        bedroom and the little guy with the
        glasses has the other, where does
        Bear sleep?

                        J.J.

        Anywhere he wants.

(BEAR CROSSES TO THE REFRIGERATOR - WILLONA
MOVES IN FRONT OF SOFA, THELMA FOLLOWS)

                    THELMA
        Look, Willona, there's nothing to worry
        about. The four of us are just roommates.
(IN THE KITCHEN - BEAR HAS REFRIGERATOR DOOR OPEN)

                    BEAR
        Isn't there anything to eat in this house?
(ALVIN ENTERS FROM BEDROOM)
                    ALVIN
(HE CROSSES TO BEAR)
        Bear, don't touch my frog!
                    J.J.
        Frog? In the refrigerator?
                    ALVIN
(CROSSING TO THELMA)
        Sure. I'm a biology major. Would
        you like to meet Thor, my tarantula?
(ALVIN EXITS TO BEDROOM, WILLONA JUMPS ON SOFA)
                    J.J.
        I'll see you downstairs.
(MOVES TO GO)
                    KAREN
(CROSSING TO STOP J.J.)
        You mean to tell me the big advertising
        genius is afraid of a little bitty spider?
                    J.J.
        The only thing with eight legs I want
        to meet is the Pointer Sisters.
(EXIT J.J. - KAREN CROSSES BEHIND SOFA LEFT)

                    WILLONA
(CROSSING TO DOOR - THELMA FOLLOWS)
    Maybe I better be going, too. Thelma,
    get your rest, don't neglect your studies...
    eat the right food, be sure and call -
                    THELMA
    Willona, you sound just like a mother.
                    WILLONA
    I do? That's terrible. Wait a minute -
    I am a mother! And us mothers have a
    very strong union.
                    THELMA
    Willona, I love you.
                    WILLONA
    I love you, too. Now you take care, hear?
(SHE EXITS - THELMA MOVES TO CHAIR - STAGE LEFT -
ENTER ALVIN WITH HIS TARANTULA IN A GLASS JAR)
                    ALVIN
(CROSSING DOWN TO END OF SOFA LEFT)
    This is Thor...Hey, where'd everyone go?
(BEAR COMES IN FROM KITCHEN)
                    BEAR
(CROSSING TO ALVIN)
    I'm hungry. Don't we have <u>anything</u>
    to eat?
(HE EYES THE SPIDER. ALVIN CLUTCHES THE JAR
AND EXITS TO BEDROOM - BEAR FOLLOWS)

                    KAREN
(SHE PICKS UP PHONE)

    Thelma, our room is a mess. Why don't
    you get started on it. While I make
    a few phone calls.

                    THELMA
(MOVING UPSTAGE)

    At last...

(TURNS DOWNSTAGE)

    a place of my own.

DISSOLVE TO:

DAZED (handwritten annotation)

ACT TWO

SCENE TWO

INT. EVANS APARTMENT - THREE WEEKS LATER - EARLY EVENING

(THREE WEEKS LATER. WILLONA AND PENNY ARE IN THE KITCHEN COOKING AT THE STOVE. WILLONA IS WORKING OVER A LARGE POT, PENNY, A LARGE APRON TIED AROUND HER, IS READING THE RECIPE TO HER OUT OF A NEWSPAPER. MICHAEL IS SETTING THE TABLE.)

          PENNY

...Add one teaspoon of salt.

          WILLONA

One teaspoon of salt. Got it.

          PENNY

Willona, why don't we just move in with J.J. and Michael? We're here every night.

          WILLONA

Honey, with J.J. holding down a job and Michael going to school, someone's got to cook for them.

          PENNY

Isn't Thelma ever coming home?

          MICHAEL

She's happy where she is, Penny.

          WILLONA

That's right, she has her own friends, her own life.

          PENNY

Well, she's been gone three weeks and I wish I could tell her I miss her.

30.

WILLONA

We all miss her, but it's important that we don't let her know.

PENNY

Why not?

MICHAEL

We don't want her to <u>think</u> we miss her.

PENNY

Why not?

MICHAEL

Because that would make her unhappy.

PENNY

I don't understand.

WILLONA

That's because you're not a grownup.

PENNY

Boy, life is a lot more simple when you're a kid.

WILLONA

Back to the cooking...What comes next?

PENNY

A quarter teaspoon of pepper.

WILLONA

A quarter teaspoon pepper...Uh-huh.

PENNY

A dash of hot sauce...

WILLONA

Dash of hot sauce.

PENNY

And stir until --

WILLONA

Stir until what?

PENNY

Stir until continued on page six.

WILLONA

Well, turn to page six.

PENNY

There is no page six.

WILLONA

What do we do now?

PENNY

What do you mean <u>we</u>, Betty Crocker?

(PENNY REMOVES HER APRON)

WILLONA

You little devil...

(HUGS HER. THELMA ENTERS)

THELMA

Hi, everyone!

(PENNY RUNS TO GREET THELMA WITH OPEN ARMS)

PENNY

Thelma!

THELMA

(HUGGING HER)

I was in the neighborhood so I thought I'd drop by and collect the rest of my things. How is everybody doing?

WILLONA
(CROSSING BEHIND J.J.)

Everything's just fine. How about you?

THELMA

Great. Couldn't be better. I bet things aren't the same around here without me.

PENNY

They sure aren't. We -

WILLONA
(CROSSING BETWEEN PENNY AND THELMA)

What Penny means is, we haven't noticed. We've all been so busy.

MICHAEL

For the first time in my life I've got a bed to myself.

THELMA

Well, I see you're about to eat. Maybe I came by at a bad time.

WILLONA

Thelma, don't be silly. There's enough to share.

THELMA

No, no. I've got dinner waiting for me at the apartment, anyway.
(CROSSES TO BEDROOM)
I'll just get my things.
(THELMA EXITS TO BEDROOM)

WILLONA

Penny, go ahead and start serving.

(J.J. ENTERS FROM BEDROOM, WITH THELMA ON HIS HEELS)

THELMA

Come back here, J.J.! What have you done to my room?

J.J.

I've given it something it's never had before...class.

THELMA

You call Lola Falana on the ceiling class? And what's that fake fur doing on the wall?

J.J.

Fake? I'll have you know that's genuine imitation rat skin.

THELMA

Where's my bed? What happened to the rest of my things? Everything's gone.

WILLONA

(CROSSING TO J.J.)

Nothing's gone. We put it in storage down in the basement.

J.J.

It was cluttering up my room.

THELMA

What do you mean your room? Listen J.J... You're right. It is your room now...

(MORE)

                    THELMA (CONT'D)
            Well, I've got to run.
    (SHE MOVES TO DOOR -)
                    WILLONA
    (CROSSING TO THELMA, PENNY FOLLOWS)
            Thelma, are you sure you won't stay
            for dinner?
                    THELMA
            No, I've really got to be going.
            I'll...call.
    (THEY AD LIB GOODBYES - THELMA EXITS)
                    PENNY
            Oh, boy. We miss Thelma and we didn't
            tell her.
    (TURNS TO OTHERS)
            And I bet she misses us and she didn't
            tell us...
    (TO WILLONA)
            Are you sure you grown ups know what
            you're doing?
    DISSOLVE TO:

ACT TWO

SCENE THREE

INT. THELMA'S APARTMENT - THAT NIGHT

(A LITTLE LATER. KAREN AND ALVIN ARE AT KITCHEN TABLE. THELMA ENTERS, STEPS OVER THE CLUTTER)

          THELMA

Well, I'm home.

(CROSSES TO THEM)

          KAREN

It's about time. You missed a great dinner, but we saved you some.

          THELMA

Good, I'm hungry. Where is it?

          KAREN

Bear ate it.

          THELMA

Again?

(KAREN EXITS TO BEDROOM)

          ALVIN

Thelma, your share of this week's grocery bill comes to fifteen dollars and ninety cents.

          THELMA

For what? I didn't eat anything.

          ALVIN

Look, we all take our chances with Bear.

THELMA
(CROSSING TO SOFA)
Never mind. I've got to study anyway.
(SITS DOWN WITH A BOOK. BEAR ENTERS FROM
BEDROOM WITH A CASSETTE PLAYER, DANCING TO
THE MUSIC - HE CROSSES DOWN PAST SOFA LEFT
THEN AROUND TO SOFA RIGHT)

THELMA (CONT'D)
Bear, I'm trying to study. Can't you do that somewhere else?

BEAR
I go where the music takes me.
(THELMA SLAMS HER BOOK SHUT. BEAR DANCES INTO BATHROOM)

ALVIN
(CROSSING TO SIT ON SOFA ARM LEFT)
Thelma, your share of this month's phone bill comes to twenty-three dollars and --

THELMA
That's impossible. I didn't call Bowlie, Oklahoma. Or anywhere else long-distance.

ALVIN
(RISES)
We split all bills equally four ways.

Good Times, Ain't We Lucky We Got 'Em: Memoir of an American Sweetheart

THELMA

(RISES)

How can I use the phone if I can't even find it?

(CROSSES UPSTAGE LEFT)

Look at this place! I cleaned it from top to bottom before I left this morning.

ALVIN

(CROSSING UPSTAGE RIGHT)

And you did a good job, too.

THELMA

(CROSSING TO HIM)

Look, Paul is coming over any min. Do you think there's a possibility that someone else could clean up this place for once!

ALVIN

You don't have to shout.

THELMA

Who's shouting.

(ALVIN CROSSES TO SIT AT TABLE - THELMA CROSSES TO BATHROOM. THE DOOR IS LOCKED)

Bear! Get out of the bathroom.

(BEAR COMES OUT FROM THE BATHROOM DANCING. THELMA TAKES THE CASSETTE PLAYER FROM HIM AND SHUTS IT OFF. HE CONTINUES DANCING ALL THE WAY INTO KITCHEN)

SFX: KNOCK ON DOOR

(THELMA CROSSES AND ANSWERS IT. IT'S PAUL, HOLDING A BOX OF CANDY)

                    PAUL
            Hi, Thelma.
                    THELMA
            Paul! Come in.
(HE ENTERS AND LOOKS AROUND)
                    PAUL
            I like your new place...I think. I
            brought you a little housewarming gift.
(GIVES CANDY TO HER)
                    THELMA
            Wow! Chocolate Cherries.
(SHE CROSSES TO SOFA - PAUL FOLLOWS)
                    BEAR
            Chocolate Cherries!
                    THELMA
            Come sit down.
(THELMA AND PAUL SIT DOWN ON THE SOFA. BEAR
AND ALVIN CROSS AND SIT ON EITHER SIDE OF THEM)
                    BEAR
(GRABBING BOX OF CANDY)
            Chocolate Cherries! Have some, Alvin.
                    ALVIN
(TAKING SOME CANDY)
            Don't mind if I do.
                    THELMA
(TAKING BOX FROM BEAR)
            Now, will you get out of here!
(BEAR AND ALVIN EXIT TO BEDROOM. KAREN ENTERS
FROM THE BEDROOM, WEARING A DIFFERENT BLOUSE -
THELMA'S)

                            KAREN
(CROSSING TO PAUL)
        Thelma, you didn't tell me we were
        having company.
(SITS ON SOFA ARM)
        Haven't we met somewhere before?
                            PAUL
        I don't know. You look familiar.
                            THELMA
(RISING)
        She ought to. She's wearing my...
        blouse...take that off!
                            KAREN
(RISING)
        If you insist...
(STARTS TO UNBUTTON)
                            THELMA
        Oh, come on, not `here!
(KAREN SITS WHERE THELMA SAT)
                            KAREN
        Hi, I'm Karen. Fly me.
                            PAUL
(PICKS UP CANDY)
        Uh...would you like a piece of candy?
                            KAREN
        Oh, Chocolate Cherries with the gooey
        centers!
(TAKES BOX OF CANDY)
        Did you bring them just for me?
(THELMA YANKS KAREN TO HER FEET)

                    THELMA
        No, he didn't, but if you don't get
        out of here, I'll have something just
        for you.
                    PAUL
(RISES)
        I better be going.
(MOVES TO GO)
                    THELMA
(CROSSING TO PAUL)
        Paul, wait.
(A FRANTIC ALVIN ENTERS WITH AN EMPTY JAR)
                    ALVIN
(CROSSING TO THELMA)
        Thor's gone! Has anybody seen my
        tarantula?
(EXITS TO BEDROOM)
                    PAUL
        I'm going.
(MOVES TO DOOR)
        Thelma, I'll call you.
(EXITS)
                    KAREN
        He's cute. A little shy, but cute.
                    THELMA
(CROSSING TO KAREN)
        Karen, I don't dig you flirting with my
        boy friend!

Good Times, Ain't We Lucky We Got 'Em: Memoir of an American Sweetheart

                    KAREN
         Look, baby, in this pad we share everything.
                    THELMA
         Good, then maybe you'd like to share
         some chocolate cherries!
(THELMA SHOVES KAREN ONTO THE COUCH, SHE FALLS
ON THE CANDY - KAREN EXITS TO BEDROOM)

SFX: KNOCK ON DOOR

(THELMA CROSSES TO THE DOOR. IT'S J.J.
WITH A BOX)
                    THELMA (CONT'D)
         J.J., what are you doing here?
                    J.J.
(HE ENTERS)
         Here's your stuff from the basement.
         You're lucky the rats only ate part of it.
(HE HANDS HER THE BOX. SHE TAKES IT AND STARTS
TO CRY)
                    THELMA
         Oh, J.J.!
                    J.J.
         I know I have this uncanny effect on
         women, but Thelma, you're my sister.
(SHE DROPS THE BOX ON HIS FEET. J.J.'S FACE
REACTS WHILE COMFORTING THELMA)
         There, there, Thelma...tell brother
         J what's ailing you.

THELMA
(CROSSING TO SOFA - J.J. FOLLOWS)
J.J.......I'm a failure.
(SITS ON SOFA ARM)

J.J.
Thelma, how can you say that? You're in college, you've got a job, you're on your own and if that weren't enough, you are the blood relative of an ebony prince...namely, me!

THELMA
J.J., I guess I was wrong. I just wasn't ready to try my wings.

J.J.
Hold on, girl. This nest may not be the right one for you. Let's face it - you're got some strange cuckoos living here.

(ALVIN ENTERS FROM THE BEDROOM AND CROSSES TO THE PHONE)

THELMA
It's not just that. I miss being home. I left two people I love to move in with the Three Stooges! You don't need a key to get into this room — you need a whip and chair!

ALVIN
(INTO PHONE)
Hello, police. I'd like to report a missing spider.

```
                        43.

              J.J.
(LOOKS DOWN)
     Hey man, either I've found your
     spider or this shirt is taking itself
     to the laundry.
              ALVIN
(HANGS UP PHONE - CROSSES TO PICK UP SHIRT
IN FRONT OF SOFA)
     Thor! Come to papa.
(ALVIN PICKS UP THE SHIRT THEN EXITS TO BEDROOM.
THELMA CROSSES IN FRONT OF SOFA - J.J. FOLLOWS)
              J.J.
     Look, Thelma, I never thought I'd say
     this, but I've finally tasted someone's
     cooking that is worse than yours....
     Willona's. Would you come back home?
              THELMA
     You don't want me. You're just saying
     that.
              J.J.
     No, I mean it. We miss you. Thelma,
     I want you to move back home.
              THELMA
     I can't.
              J.J.
     Please.
              THELMA
     What about your trying to run my life?
```

I don't believe this

J.J.

No more of that, Thelma. I promise.

THELMA
(MOVING HIM BACK TOWARDS DOOR)

Good. Now get this... start peeling that Fur off the Wall, get Lola Falana off the ceiling, get my things back in my room where they belong.

(PICKS UP BOX - HANDS IT TO J.J.)

Because J.J... I'm coming home!

FADE OUT:

END OF ACT TWO

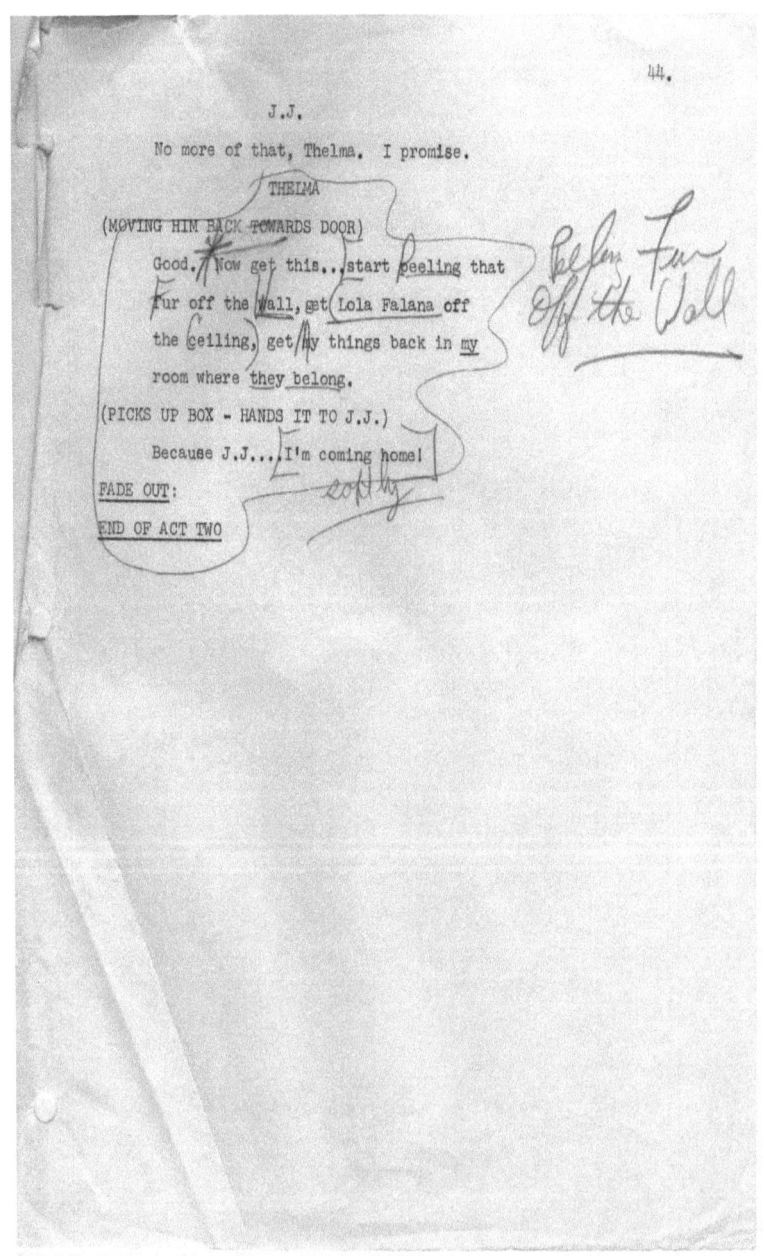

Peel the Fur Off the Wall

softly

About Brittany Rose

Brittany Rose is a fourth-year medical student with a deep passion for both medicine and family. She navigates the demanding path of her studies while embracing the joy of family life alongside her husband and their daughter, Eulilia. Together, they treasure cozy movie nights and lively game nights filled with laughter.

Besides her love for family, Brittany has a strong connection to nature, expressed through her butterfly collection. She enjoys traveling, exploring new places, and trying unique cuisines at different restaurants. A significant experience for Brittany was helping her mother, BernNadette Stanis, write her memoir, *Good Times, Ain't We Lucky We Got 'Em: Memoir of an American Sweetheart*, where she witnessed her mother's joy in sharing cherished memories. Through these experiences, Brittany finds beauty in the love, laughter, and good times that define her journey.